SKY MAN

SKY MAN

A Celebration of Life

The Life of Skylar Page,
a gift from The Father,
as told by his father,

Mike Page

Hurricane Hill Publishing

Hurricane Hill Publishing
An Imprint of Hurricane Hill LLC
Augusta, KS

The stories and incidents in this book are based on true events in the life of Skylar Page. Some are documented and some are told based on the best recollection of the writer. Other than family and public figures, the names used in the stories have been changed. No story involving anyone that is mentioned in this book should be taken negatively; as the stories are meant to be positive. So many people have had a positive influence on Skylar's life; unfortunately they are not all mentioned here. Some may recognize themselves from certain stories. By changing the names, they can choose whether to acknowledge themselves as the positive influence written about.

ISBN 978-0-692-82399-6

Printed in the United States of America

Cover Design: The cover was designed by Ryan Keefover. Ryan has known Skylar since Sky's birth. The night sky fading to light theme is by the author. It represents Sky's life path from darkness to ever increasing light and hope. An eternal revelation that is available to everyone.

This book is dedicated to people worldwide considered to be handicapped or to have special needs. It is also dedicated to all that individually or as a family care for them; both professionally and on a charitable basis. God Bless You.

The Celebration

Author's Note

Sky Man is really a story about celebrating life. It is a true compilation of many of the events in my son Skylar's life. The bigger message however is about celebrating life in both its simplicity and complexity. No matter where you came from or how life comes at you, it is your life and it should be celebrated. I've learned that Special Needs people like Skylar are often ignored, mistreated and shunned. Although they come in all shapes, sizes, ethnicities, economic statuses, levels of intelligence and uniqueness as everyone else; they are still often separated and mistreated. It has resulted in my coming to the conclusion that the prejudice towards Special Needs People is the greatest prejudice that still needs to be overcome in this world. Sky Man is not a perfectly written book. As in life, in the book he is called both Sky and Skylar at various times with little thought about which to use. The book is compiled and written to the best of my ability to tell a real story. It is intentionally not overly edited for perfection in grammar, layout, or spelling. After all, it is about a young man that many would consider flawed. Well, we are all flawed and none of us are perfect; thus a perfect manuscript is not provided. It is my hope that you will experience a variety of human emotions by reading about just a few of our experiences recounted in this book. Perhaps this young man's story and the effects he has had on our family's lives will encourage you and make you think about your life and family. I hope it encourages you first of all to minimize your prejudices toward accepting people of all conditions. I hope it encourages you to better your own life and dream about the possibilities in your future. I hope it encourages you to live life to the fullest while helping others. I also hope it makes you think. Think about helping others less fortunate. Think about your life maybe not being all so bad. Think about your purpose in life. Think about your eternal future. Finally, I hope you will find it entertaining and worth your time to read. Sky's story may not be the most tear jerking, the funniest, most spiritual or best written story you will read, but nevertheless, I think it will be entertaining.

Prologue

Skylar Page was born on May 25, 1995. I think I heard it stated in song lyrics sung many years ago, "He came into the world in the usual way". Sky, as we call him, was a beautiful baby boy, perfect in every way. Soon however, he was diagnosed with a heart defect that threatened his very existence. When he grew stronger and if he survived his heart could be repaired. This life saving procedure was completed when he was 10 months old. Sky was also soon after birth diagnosed with something else that many would consider a birth defect. He was diagnosed with Trisomy 21, a form of Down Syndrome. It's not that something's missing. Actually he has three 21st chromosomes in the DNA make up instead of the most common, two. Not something missing, but something extra. Not something ordinary but something extraordinary. I believe it's a gifted ability to see the world in a different light. A God given ability to love and accept all people just as they are, an ability to truly care for them from the heart; just like family.

Over the years, Sky has had his struggles but through it

all he has been a source of inspiration. Some of the funniest and most thoughtful comments and events we have experienced have come through him. His life also brought us into contact with many special needs individuals. Sky helped us open our eyes to more people in the world with special needs. We were like horses having their blinders removed. The needs were always there, it just took Sky to help us see them. Sky has accomplished a lot of things that we never dreamed would happen including attending college, delivering a short sermon at a national event, and driving a car. Safely driving, I might add. Sky feels a need to help others while building a solid future for his self. He knows that God has gifted him to help and inspire others. As he stated in his Short Sermon, Jeremiah 29:11 says:

"For I know the plans I have for you,' says The Lord, 'Plans to prosper you and not to harm you, Plans to give you a hope and a future." NIV

This has become a standard theme in Sky's life, along with a few closing lines from that sermon. Words that should speak to all of us:

"Don't let others or yourself stop you from doing all that you can do. I bet that I had doubters, but I

know that God never doubted me, because He has made me LIMITLESS."

Chapter 1

The Awakening

Awakening is defined as: an act or moment of becoming suddenly aware of something.

In The Beginning

"He came into The World in the usual way." I remember thinking about those positive song lyrics, although God had orchestrated an early arrival. I'm sure, according to His Plan. You know, it is His Plan. There were a few fears that had to be overcome. Then, all seemed fine. Mom had been worried. I know Christians aren't supposed to worry, but he was five weeks early. You see Mom had lost her first child, years earlier, to Hyaline Membrane Disease. He too was five weeks early. Was there, I thought, some irony in the prior child's name having been Christian? Worry is very human. A nightmare of imagery from life to death must have been playing in Mom's mind. Like an endless loop I suppose. Again a boy. Again five weeks early. Again four days of life? Did I mention there had been thirty six hours of labor? That's a long time for a woman that I've seen deliver the most recent two children in forty-six minutes and ninety minutes respectively. I had thought that I should have graduated Lamaze Class as Valedictorian. It sure wasn't the same this time. The Doctor became rather concerned too. He had said that he was going to do a Caesarean section if the baby didn't come soon. I guess that's fine, but not for a woman that has already brought five children into the world in the "old-fashioned way". Really, she had done it God's way. He's not old-fashioned you know. He's the same yesterday today, and forever.

A Miracle

Miracles come through prayer. I'm convinced of it. Also, you may have to wait. Waiting isn't a bad thing. We wait if we want hot food. We wait in line for the best tickets. We wait for the right restaurant table. Some even wait for the right person to marry and spend their life with. Many of life's best things are the result of waiting but, believe me, the prayer thing helps. My friend Daniel had just "happened" to show up at the hospital. I believe he was there for me. Surely, the baby wouldn't look like him. If so, this would be a whole different story. Well, Danny is a man of prayer. When I tell him what the doctor has said, he asks that we go in the hall and pray. You know what happened? It wasn't long and that baby started to come, "The Old-Fashioned Way". I didn't even have to suffer the green meconium water cannon that erupted on me when my wife was birthing our daughter. So much for that waiting thing being good, prayer was even better and sped up the process. Better yet, there is surfactant available if needed. I had told the doctor about mom worrying about the possibility of Hyaline Membrane Disease. He said that losing a baby from that is a thing of the past. If Hyaline Membrane Disease is present; they give them surfactant, to lubricate their lungs. He said it is derived from baby cows. Now that is a miracle! At least I thought it was, but a more exciting miracle was soon to appear.

Excitement

It's a boy! He's beautiful. Of course, all parents think their babies are cute. Not only is he beautiful in our eyes, but he is a perfect miracle. The Apgar score confirms it. That takes away some of our concern, partially due to mom's age. When pregnant with our daughter 5 years earlier, my wife had taken an alpha-fetoprotein test. We were told it can determine if the baby may have Down syndrome. It wasn't a very accurate test method at the time. Her test came back positive for possibly carrying a child with Down syndrome. She wouldn't do any further testing as it could harm the baby. Well we didn't have a Down child, just an ornery one. I'm sure that when faced with it, we had prayed to not have a handicapped child. I guess we thought our prayer was miraculously answered. Later, I might question that.

Questions

I first noticed that he is sticking his tongue out a lot. It seems rather long. But, he has been through a difficult labor. His ears look normal. No Simian creases in his hands, although the Pediatrician has them. No abnormal features. He's not Down syndrome. At least none of the Doctors think so. I don't think so. He is our son and a perfect miracle after all. He's got the score to prove it. Then something changed in that room. When I first noticed, it was subtle. Mom's crying, rather sobbing. It's not your normal Mother's cry of happiness. I've seen that cry before. This is different. Does she know something? I may not have seen it, but our lives would never be the same after this event. Though I didn't think about it at the time, God had possibly been preparing me for this many years prior. As a child there were two periods in my life where my best friends were physically handicapped. I knew they were different but I didn't think of them as different or treat them as such. When I think about it now I remember that they really didn't have many friends and were sometimes made fun of. "Soppit" was the nickname given to one of my friends. Not because of his partially humped back and permanently sideways leaning head, but also because he had a speech impediment. He couldn't say "Stop it" when kids were mistreating him, so they nicknamed him. I'm not sure exactly why, but he became my best friend while living in that neighborhood. I didn't really think of him as different. He was just my friend. If my son was to be different, I now think that God allowed me a time to nurture compassion for the handicapped in my early youth. Childhood is a time when all of us really are vulnerable and more accepting. Of course it doesn't take long before life changes us. I think a multitude of things transform us in to not accepting or being receptive to various groups of people. Maybe I was given Divine training; a preview of what The Bible means when saying we must become like little children to enter the Kingdom of Heaven. Of course over the years my mind would be prejudiced too. I would need something or some event to bring me back to that childlike state. Perhaps I was about to receive what I needed physically, emotionally and spiritually; an awakening. The Awakening of a miracle in his father's eyes and heart had begun.

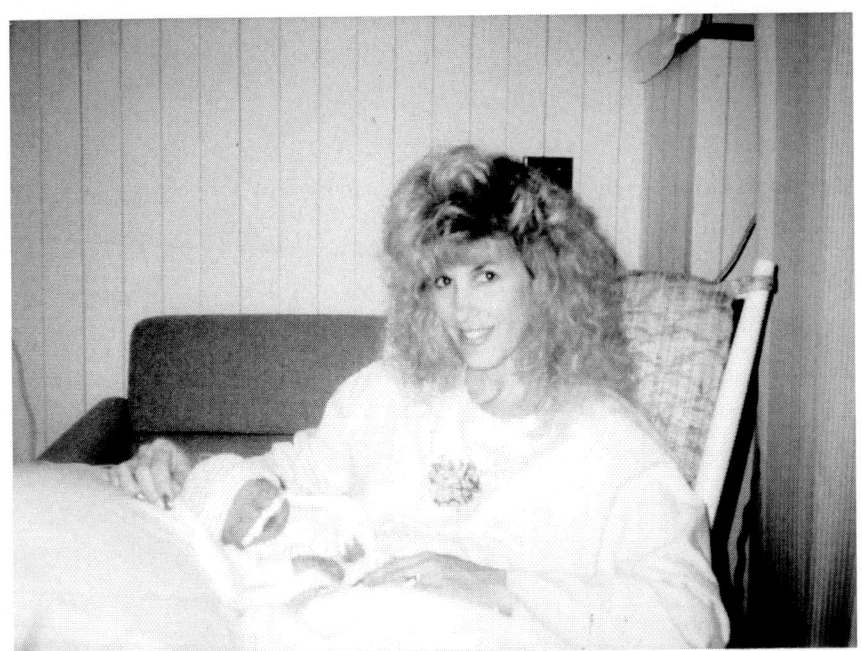

Mom (Paula) and Sky shortly after birth and long labor.

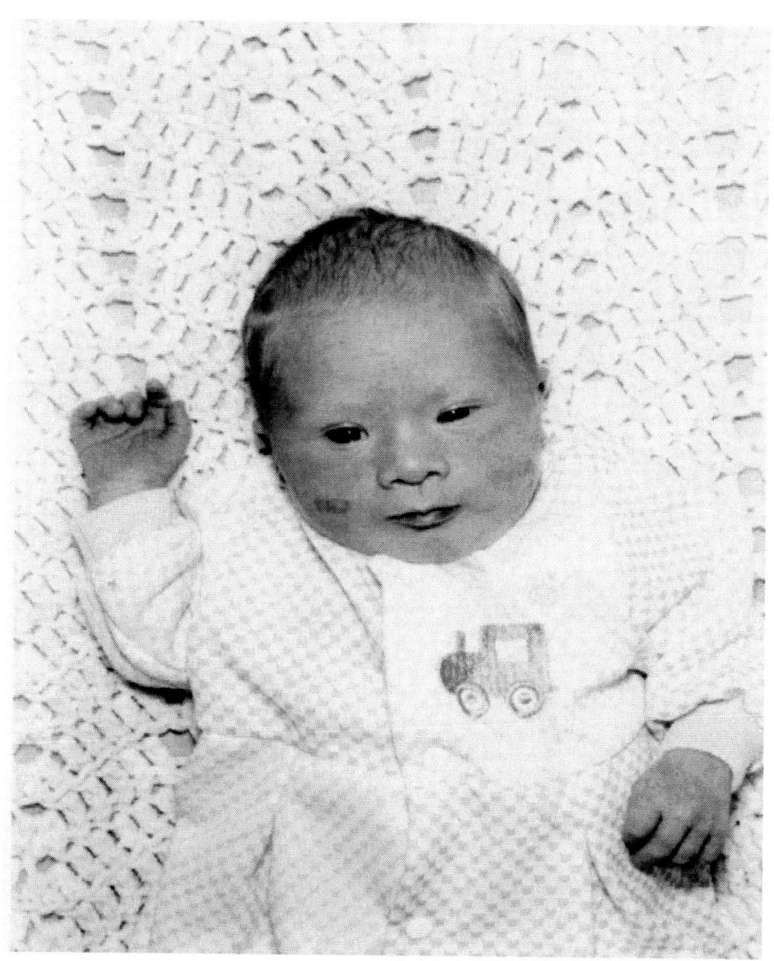

Skylar as a new born. Looking pretty normal I thought.

Chapter 2

The Darkness

Darkness is described as: the total or partial absence of light, wickedness or evil.

A Message

It was standard procedure to take a premature baby to the special care nursery. This really didn't cause me any alarm but there was still a lingering concern with Mom. Being an optimist, sometimes to a fault, I was rather relaxed in an odd sort of way. The nurses did after all do pretty much everything for you. My fatherly role was to hold the baby, help feed him, and contemplate my portion of the inevitable medical bills. This was further complicated by the fact that I was on the threshold of going through one of the, soon to be, most horrific business times in my life. I remember thinking; I sure love this baby. He needs me. Little did I realize at the time just how much his future would multiply this in so many directions. I really didn't know him, but he was a part of me. I do know I really cared about him, but I was also enjoying the break from the business world. It was probably selfish to be resting. At least I was resting with him. Mom or I never left his side. I remember an odd thing happened during one of the night shifts. I know I wasn't asleep and it wasn't a dream. Mom could stand witness to this. In the middle of the night a nurse came in to check the baby. Our time with her was rather short and I don't remember her doing a whole lot. What I remember is what she said, "special kids are given to special people". Well, thank you, I thought. Most likely, I said it too; probably meant it. I'm sure she must have been talking about my wife. Then she was gone. This was the only time we saw her. She wasn't the regular nurse. Her visit was brief as if she were sent specifically to give us a simple message. I tried to find out later who she was, maybe get a name so she could be properly thanked. I was taking her words as a compliment now. Finding her was to no avail. No one seemed to know her or why she would have even been in our area. You can draw your own conclusions. I choose to believe in angels. I believe in God sending a word when we need it, even when we don't realize it's needed. Sometimes it comes from a friend or someone we know. Sometimes it can't be explained. I'd soon know how much I needed that word.

Complications

I can't recall who first noticed that the baby's arms and legs had a slight blue tone to them. I'm sure it wasn't me. Most likely mom noticed. She was an expert not only at birthing babies but also at just being a darn good mom. The kind everyone should get. I should clarify that she was an expert at birthing, "her own babies", unlike our fellow Wichitan in Gone With The Wind. After all she had birthed five of her own babies already. This latest "blue" revelation started a whole battery of tests. It also heightened Mom's concerns. She had known something was wrong. Maybe this was what she had sensed shortly after delivery. The first thing was to test the heart. The possible heart problem also raised the concerns of Down syndrome. Things started moving rather fast. It wasn't so relaxing anymore to be in the hospital. We were told that over 40 percent of Down syndrome kids are born with heart defects. The preliminary tests on his heart were not very positive. Eventually we were told that he had a full AV canal defect. My understanding is that this is a situation where the heart valves are not formed completely and you either have just one or two chambers in the heart. We were also asked to authorize genetic testing to see whether he had Down syndrome. We approved this, but not until after being told that the tests had no health risk to the baby. It would probably be better to know now, so we would know what to expect. Either way, we had no idea of what to expect. I mean what can prepare you for a handicapped child? Probably only another handicapped child could. At least this may be our only one. Some people have more than one child with a defect. We should probably be counting our blessings.

Rest When You're Dead

Thirty days for the results of the genetic test. That's a long time to wait for a potentially catastrophic result. I mean this is the kind of thing that changes peoples' lives. Some people might have chosen to (legally?) terminate this child. I wouldn't have, so I'm really not too worried about the result. He's my son. A lot of things change peoples' lives; marriage, death, the birth of a first child, job loss; the list goes on and on. I believe that you play life's cards the way they are dealt. I didn't want any more tragedy in my life after having lost my parents at a relatively young age. I knew however that tragedy often precedes triumph. At least in the dictionary it does. It would be years however before I really understood how true this was. Not much time had passed before we were getting a lot of information and instructions on what we would have to do for him because of the heart defect. It would be necessary to feed him often, at minimum every two hours. This was because he tired easily due to his weak heart; which made it hard to eat. We would have to give him medicines to help lower the pressure on his heart and minimize its enlargement, as he got older. If, he could make it to at least six months old before going into congestive heart failure, his survival odds from surgery would greatly increase. Ideally, if having the surgery done at ten to twelve months old, his survival chances would increase from seventy percent to ninety five percent. What else could complicate our lives? I would not have considered lack of sleep. Sleep is a precious commodity with any newborn. With ours, this would be an understatement.

I Am

Did I mention he needed a name? That's right. They won't even let you out of the hospital without naming your child. You'd think they'd want to just charge you for the defective product you've just received and get you out of there. Well they wouldn't. We were always able to name the other kids pretty quickly. I think we had their names picked out before they were born. I don't know what it was but we just couldn't come up with a name. Maybe we would just stay in the hospital. Maybe not! Well, let's get this kid a name.

Who does he look like? I thought about what my Grandma Ryan always said when somebody asked that question about a baby. She'd say "he just looks like him". She was right. He does look just like him, or..........maaaybe, like a rubber chicken. He's not looking real healthy. Maybe Foghorn Leghorn would work for a name. I know Mom wouldn't go for that. Maybe Schnauzer which one of my friends swore he wanted to name his daughter. I couldn't even suggest that. Anyway that was intended as a girl's name. Whatever we name him, he's stuck with it for life. Oh, I'm sure there will be nicknames but a given name is important. I still don't know where his first name came from. His middle name was like mine, from a great grandpa I didn't know, whose first name was Giles. We couldn't name him Giles. That sounded like a butler or chauffeur. Maybe his first name was just meant to be; sent down from the great I Am. We have to tell the hospital. Okay, we've got a name; it's official. Now, let us outta here! Let's take Skylar Harding Page home.

Going Home

Home is where the heart is, literally in our case. The heart that doesn't work right is at our home. So is the sick kid that needs fed every hour or two around the clock. This is tough. How do people deal with a sick child? It's a good thing that I didn't know we wouldn't sleep much for a year or two. Can you take a kid back and get a refund? Maybe it's a good thing that I've become a Christian and changed my ways. I'm sure it's a good thing that I married the woman I did. Her mothering instincts will help me to do the right thing.

Feed him, Lasix, Digoxin, feed him, Lasix, Digoxin, try to work; the pattern pretty much keeps repeating itself. Mom did a lot more of it than me. A few months in he seems to be doing fairly well, considering. Other things however weren't going well at all. Our business was experiencing difficult times and we were tied up in a job that involved many managerial hours. It was also starting to affect our cash flow. My wife's dad was also experiencing some health problems. We had three other kids at home, a sixteen year old, an eight year old and a five year old, that also needed our attention. Then there was Skylar's first bout with pneumonia requiring hospitalization. This was the first of two that would occur prior to his heart being worked on. It helped that one of his hospital nurses was a lady who attended our church. Again, it provided a little reassurance that we were not alone in our circumstances. I remember holding the little rubber device between my figures and tapping his back and chest for what seemed like hours, attempting to help break up his chest congestion. It looked a lot easier when done by the respiratory therapists in the hospital. It looked easier when mom did it too, particularly in the middle of the night. It wasn't the easiest to do but I'm sure that parents of asthmatic children have faced similar but more difficult tasks. Like I said though, in life, you just play the cards you're dealt. You can always look around and see others who have been dealt worse hands and be thankful that "your cards" aren't so bad. It is best not to think about the tasks but just do them the best you can. I can assure you, they will pass. In time the memory of the tasks won't seem so difficult or much of a price to have paid for the joy you will experience. I've heard it said that joy comes in the morning. It does, and morning comes when you awake and realize that joy; joy from the life you are caring for.

Something Extra?

I'm not sure exactly when the genetic test results came back. We had been told that there were only two types of Down syndrome; Trisomy 21 and Mosaic. My understanding was that people with Down syndrome are actually not lacking something genetically but have something extra. With Trisomy 21, the individual has three copies of the genes on the twenty first chromosomes in every cell of their DNA make up; in lieu of a "normal person" having two. An individual that is Mosaic only has three gene copies on the twenty first chromosomes in a portion of their cells. The Mosaic individuals tend to have less mental deficiencies and function at a higher level of learning. Because of Skylar's high Apgar score and not having most of the Down syndrome characteristics, I believe everyone assumed if he were diagnosed with Down syndrome, he would be Mosaic. The heart defect had made it more likely that he would be diagnosed with Down syndrome; which type would be one more card to be dealt. It really shouldn't have made any difference what the results were, but it did. I think it is a human trait to hope for the best or what we think is going to be the best. I think it is also a trait with many to expect the worst. Both are most likely based upon what we think will make things the easiest for us. Easy however, does not always result in what is best for us. Now, I believe that I should not have been concerned about the test either way. All I should have cared about was loving my son and helping him to be the best that he could be. No different than for any other child, regardless of their individual strengths and weaknesses. Well, the tests did eventually come back. By the time they did, I don't even think we cared about the results. There were too many other things that we needed to deal with. The result we received, Trisomy 21, could be perceived by some as total darkness. As we believe, God too comes in the darkness. Just as the sun rises in the east to bring daytime light to the darkness of the night, He too will someday rise as the light in the east. We had to make a choice, give up or rise up. Though we didn't know how, we chose to hold on to the hope of our faith as our way to overcome; The Darkness.

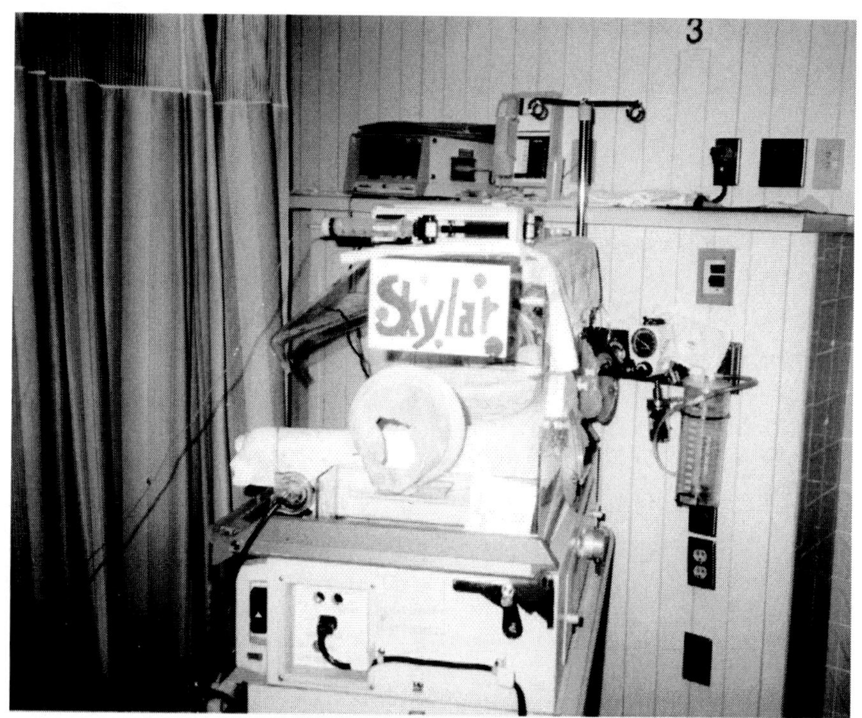

Skylar in the Special Care Nursery. This was his home when "The Angel" came to see him and encourage us.

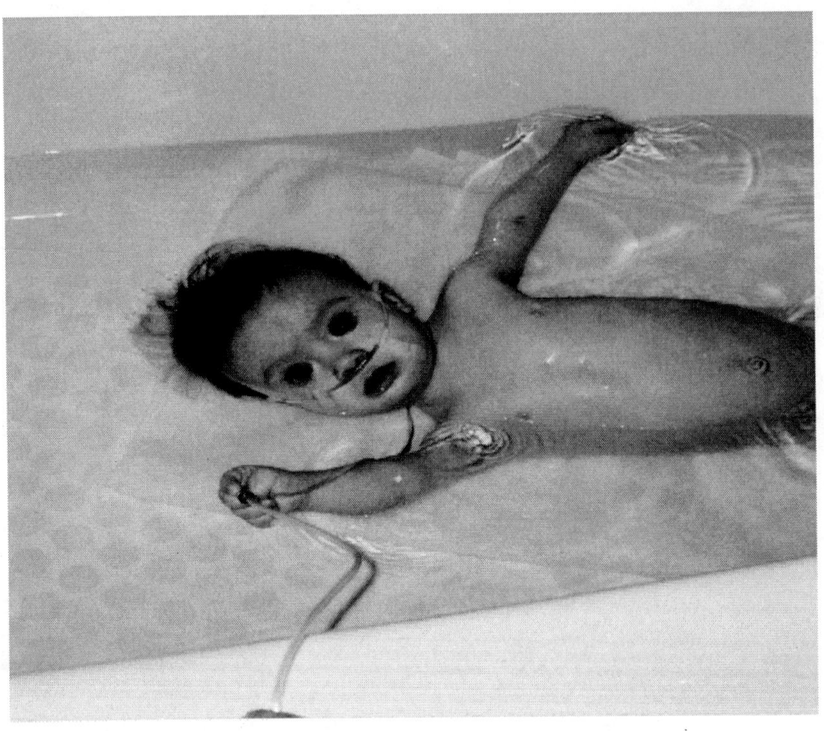

This was Skylar in his "rubber chicken" phase. Prior to heart surgery (note no zipper), he had pneumonia twice and was on oxygen often.

Chapter 3

The Light

Light is defined as: the natural agent that stimulates sight and makes things visible. It also is defined as: understanding a mystery, enlightenment.

Options

"I'm not sure exactly when it happened", seems to be a common thread with me. It's again accurate about when we decided to have Sky's condition checked at the Mayo Clinic in Rochester Minnesota. I knew Mayo was world renowned. I knew our Pastor and one of my friends had been there previously, but I imagined it difficult to get an appointment and very expensive. I'd been told that appointments were booked up for many months. Our time frame was limited. Although I'd been raised that you could do and accomplish anything, I really didn't believe the possibility of being seen by the Mayo Clinic as a potential reality. Our son's cardiologist wanted us to schedule with a

Children's Hospital where he had interned. I was sure that it was a fine facility, but I also had something inside me drawing me toward Mayo. Ultimately, I picked up the phone and called Mayo Clinic to inquire about an appointment. I was very surprised to find that we could get an appointment within a few weeks. This would put our appointment date in December. That being so easy, I encouraged my wife to have her father Loyd also make an appointment. He had been going to doctors for over a year and a half and no one could diagnose the cause of his arm bothering him. Well, he was also able to make an appointment at the same time as Skylar's. This necessitated a road trip being planned. We would get information to help us decide where to have Sky's surgery and Lloyd would get a diagnosis. Everyone would get a little peace of mind. When the appointed time neared we loaded up the SUV and we headed off for the 10 hour drive to Rochester.

Appointments

Our initial appointments were scheduled on Monday and Tuesday. The way Mayo worked was you had your initial consultation early in the week. Any needed tests or other consultations were then scheduled for the rest of the week. Typically, you would then come in on Friday for a diagnosis or final meeting to determine the next steps for treatment. Skylar's first appointment was with the cardiologist, Dr. Davidson. We had to wait a while but there were signs that apologized for your wait; saying that they liked to allow each patient the needed time with the doctor. During the appointment, Dr. Davidson apologized as he would take calls on his cell phone. I found out that these calls were ones that he felt were important concerning other patients. On some calls the patient was put through to talk to him. This was sure different from most medical facilities I had experienced. At most, you would never be able to reach the doctor immediately unless maybe you were their family member. In most instances you would not even be able to reach a nurse but reduced to leaving a message for a return call. I was impressed. This seemed more like how I would do things in my business although it is definitely less important and doesn't involve potentially life threatening situations. I'm not knocking the medical profession or singling them out. I'm just stating a fact and making a distinction about a difference that I noted at a unique facility. Come to think of it, many churches are similar when you're an outsider trying to reach the Main Man in charge; and their purpose involves even more important eternal issues. Maybe I should just move on. Dr. Davidson discussed the way Mayo does things and scheduled additional tests for Skylar. Multiple tests were performed on him that week. I felt like we were being treated like going to the doctor when I was a kid.

I felt less rushed; more personal attention and more relaxed. I was becoming more comfortable with Mayo and our path we would have to walk.

Consider the Odds

It was an interesting and informational week. As a business person, I was impressed by several things. One was that all doctors at Mayo had to be asked to practice there. You could not just apply. Secondly, we were told, all doctors are salaried. This way there was no financial incentive to do additional unneeded procedures. They said that it doesn't happen often but there are instances where a doctor could do something unnecessary for financial gain. When inquiring about my costs, I was told that overall their charges were 22% less on average than other clinics and hospitals. I trusted God but was also interested in statistics. I had learned previously that the chance of death from the heart procedure Skylar needed was 30% if needed in the first six months of life. It reduced to 5% if it could be delayed past 6 months and closer to a year of age. We had made it past the six month point. Mayo's death rate was even lower at 3%. Maybe dawn was coming and darkness would give way to light. Another impressive thing to me about Mayo was they would tell you their opinion of the best places in the country to have various procedures done. They even told us of two other places in the country that they felt were equals to them in the type of surgery Sky needed. They said they weren't the best at everything but hearts were one area where they excelled. I greatly appreciated their honesty and overall conservative approach. The sophisticated, sterile, and aloof academic environment that I envisioned in my mind for Mayo to be was totally dismantled that week. It seemed like an old school approach to medicine and more like going to the doctor when I was a kid. It was refreshing to deal with some of the most highly rated doctors and a world renowned clinic that made you feel like an important equal. They knew who they were and had nothing to prove.

Choices

Though I expound on the virtues of Mayo, Sky was blessed that God had provided him with amazing caring doctors at home also. When the end of the week came, we were asked if we thought we wanted the surgery done at Mayo Clinic and their affiliate, St. Mary's Hospital. The decision was not a difficult one. The conservative caring approach of the clinic, an open ICU policy allowing a parent to be at his bedside around the clock, and a 50% nurse to pediatric patient ratio during recovery at St. Mary's; all were major contributing factors in our decision. My tour of the Mayo museum and seeing a soldering iron exactly like we use for sheet metal work that was used years ago to cauterize hemorrhoids, fortunately, did not deter my decision. The choice was made. Mayo it would be.

Life and Death

We had not met the surgeon but did meet his assistant. We were told that the surgery would be performed by Dr. Fernando Pubah. The surgery would be scheduled for March of 1996 to allow Skylar to possibly grow and strengthen more. If he started to experience congestive heart failure sooner, the date would be moved up. It was a bitter sweet week. Although we were happy that we were able to secure a surgery date for Skylar, the diagnosis on my father-in-law was not so good. When called in to discuss his test results he was told he had amyotrophic lateral sclerosis; often called ALS or Lou Gehrig's disease. In most cases your father having been given a medical death sentence would be the number one thing on your mind. When you have a child possibly facing death at the same time, the scales tend to dip toward the child and the preservation of the next generation. Skylar was facing difficult odds with his diagnosis but they were much better than those of

ALS. Lou Gehrig's disease would take Loyd's life a little over seven months later.

Weighing the Cost

With Sky's surgery scheduled I started to further contemplate what our costs would be in addition to what the insurance would cover. We had been more concerned with getting the best treatment rather than worrying about the cost. Although we were facing some strange business conditions that would ultimately prove to be the toughest of our life, Sky's health was our main concern. As I looked at costs that we would have, I realized that although we were out of network and the insurer paid a lesser percentage, our out of pocket cost would be no higher than had we used a provider in our own home town. This was due to the costs resulting in reaching our maximum out of pocket expense on our health insurance policy either way. The only additional costs we would have would be our travel and lodging expenses. I considered it a miracle to get the best care for the same price.

Confirmation

This being uncharted territory for us it was a very difficult time. Like others facing tough situations you really don't have time to think about your situation. You just have to live life and take one day at a time. After all, I wasn't the one with a life threatening condition. As a parent though, I came to realize that I was carrying the same burden. Possibly, only a mother may feel it more. I know now that only our faith in God got us through it. Just when you most need it, He is The Comforter that confirms your decisions. It was sometime in January, only about a month after the Mayo decision was made that God gave us a much needed confirmation. A lady in our church, Louise, asked my wife who Skylar's doctors were. We told her Dr. Davidson and Dr. Pubah. She said she had bought a well known magazine at the grocery store and it had an article in it about the best doctors in the nation for various medical categories. A week later she brought the magazine to church. The article had only about three names in each category. Both Dr. Davidson and Dr. Pubah were listed. Not only were they listed but they were the only ones from Mayo Clinic listed in their respective categories of pediatric cardiologists and pediatric heart surgeons. On top of that it listed Dr. Pubah as the Head of Pediatric Heart Surgery at Mayo Clinic. We took this news as a divine confirmation of our decision to go to Mayo Clinic. Had we randomly been assigned two of the best doctors in the country after not even being sure we could get an appointment? I don't think so. I said that we were just dumb enough to try to get the best and God took care of the rest. Far beyond what we could ask or think. If you trust God, is it wrong to feel some relief when you get the best according to the scales of man? I don't think so, because you still need to trust God and the unique talents he has bestowed on certain individuals. If God orchestrates it, sit back and enjoy the music.

The Wait

The next few months waiting for the surgery date were a stressful time. Business was tough, a hospital stay due to Skylar having pneumonia, and praying that his heart would function well enough to make it to the scheduled surgery date. We would need to make physical, mental, and spiritual preparations for the task ahead. How do you prepare for something you've not experienced? It is facing the unknown. Just as all men must die and at some time in their life face that reality; most do not know how to prepare for it. We were facing what seemed an insurmountable obstacle that would strain every facet of our being. There was no logical way to prepare. All we could do was trust our faith and walk the path laid before us.

Preparations

While at Mayo, the doctors had told us that Skylar would need 5 pints of blood available for the surgery. We were told that either it could be obtained from the blood bank or we could give blood and have it sent to them to be held for his surgery. Skylar had a blood type of O Positive so suitable donors would need to be found. I was the only family member with the same blood type. Due to restrictions on giving more than 1 pint of blood within 56 days and the surgery date fast approaching, I would only be able to give two pints. We would need donors for the rest. People in the church stepped up and offered to give blood. Two ladies in our church and the father of one of them were of the same blood type. They graciously offered and were selected for the task. Their giving blood may not have seemed like a big task to them, but to me it was much more. I thought it was one thing for a father to sacrifice his blood for a son, but it was much more for a non-family member to do so. To me the spiritual parallel to Jesus giving his blood willingly for all mankind was of profound significance. I believe that their giving blood for Skylar is one of those things that may seem small to many, but to God, is a big thing that he justly rewards.

Taking Risks

Not long before the surgery, I gave my second pint of blood. It was complete and we would not need to have any concern about the blood Skylar would receive. It was the next day when we were notified by Mayo that additional blood was needed because one bag broke when frozen for preservation. This created a dilemma as there was not time to wait the required time period before giving another pint. With all of this preparation to not need random blood from the blood bank, we may be forced to need it anyway. I know the screening processes are excellent but this was a disappointment. I'm not sure who told me, but somewhere I had heard that with a doctor's order you could give blood sooner. Not having a physician that I regularly saw, and due to my wife just happening to have an appointment with her doctor, I had no choice. Drastic circumstances require drastic measures, so I did feel a need to visit the OBGYN. I didn't have time to make my own appointment, which would have been really awkward, so I had to go with my wife who fortunately had a regular appointment already scheduled. At her appointment, I told the doctor of my dilemma. To myself I thought, "What's the big deal?" it's an issue of blood, just different than he was used to. I figured it may help my request that he knew us. Although I was risking embarrassment to my wife and our whole family by my request, I felt it worth the risk. Later I knew it was probably because I was healthy that the order was granted.

Is It Really Worth It?

I would now be giving my third pint of blood for Skylar; two within three days. I remember that I really wasn't too worried. After all I thought of myself as a big, tough guy. The lady in charge at the Red Cross was further reassuring. She said that people many years prior gave 2 pints all the time. She said this commonly happened during war time and added that I would have no problem. The process progressed and seemed to be going pretty well. I was most of the way through when the attendant told me to raise my knees up and start pumping my feet up and down. I had been thinking I was a little light headed but maybe that was normal for me. The process ended and I asked what had happened. I was told that I had turned white as a sheet and they thought I would pass out. I was told to stay lying down for 15 minutes before going to the adjoining room for a snack and drink. I still thought I was fine but when I went to get my snack I felt a little funny. I also was cold and tired. I spent about 45 minutes waiting in a convalescent state until I felt good enough to drive home. The rest of the evening I spent watching jittery television as I was on the couch wrapped in blankets and shivering. I swear I wasn't complaining when I told my wife they had about killed me. Actually I was proud of my accomplishment as I joked that the Red Cross lady had lied to me about how easy it would be. I think I said she was probably some kind of vampire that was in charge of draining the life blood out of me. My situation however paled, literally, in comparison as I thought of the spiritual parallels that I believed in and how Jesus gave his blood for me. Had it called for me to die for my son, would I be up to the task? I thought so, but honestly couldn't be sure.

More Waiting

Eventually, the surgery date was upon us. We made the trip to Rochester with just Skylar, Paula and I. It was rare for us to travel without all of our children but this was a time when we needed to concentrate on Skylar. Our close friends would bring our other kids up once Skylar went from the ICU to a hospital room. We procured a hotel room across the street from the hospital so as to have a nearby resting place. Prior to surgery you check into the hospital and once again see the doctors for some final tests. Skylar was experiencing some chest congestion and started running a fever. We were told the surgery would have to be postponed. Tests revealed he did not have an infection but some type of virus. The doctors told us that if they treated him with antibiotics that he would be better in seven days and if they didn't treat him, he would be better in a week. In other words, the virus would have to run its course and surgery be postponed for a week. Our pastor and others had come to be with us for the surgery, but evidently that wasn't God's plan. Skylar was checked out of the hospital and we were on our own for a week. There is only so much to see in Rochester and it didn't make sense to travel home, so off to nearby Minneapolis we went. I wasn't in the right mood for The Mall of America or any other mall. Of course that was not any different than any other time in my life. Yes, I went. Other than losing a diamond ring in the snow that I inherited from my father; I don't remember much else of what we did that week of waiting. I do know one thing. I'm sure I prayed.

Questions

The following week we returned to Mayo and the

surgery was again scheduled. The night before the surgery we met the surgeon, Dr. Pubah, for the first time. Dr. Pubah was of Spanish descent and had studied at The National University in Mexico City. This was an eye opener. I wasn't prejudiced but I knew surgery was very technical and nothing like the construction business which we were in. We were more experienced with Hispanic people being known for their hard work ethic in more physically laborious jobs. Time and people's preconceptions about Skylar would later teach me to be even less stereotypical in my thinking. Currently however, I was curious about this foreign Doctor. Several things did give me comfort. I had been told that some of the best surgeons were from other countries as they often offered a more lenient legal environment to develop life saving methods. After all, the Doctor was the head of pediatric surgery at a world renowned clinic. He was in the magazine article as one of the best. Surely God had put this together. Then Dr. Pubah explained the surgery. He explained that Skylar's heart was about the size of a golf ball. He would try to use the pericardium tissue around the heart to reconstruct the middle of the heart and make two new valves. If he were able to, Skylar would probably never need heart surgery again in his life. He told us that only a small percentage of children receiving this repair develop valve leakage. This often occurs at five or six years of age, and there becomes a need to install a new valve. If Dr. Pubah could not make the repair using the pericardium, it would require the use of an artificial pig tissue valve. This type of repair would need redone approximately every ten years. Your mind goes through many emotions when trying to grasp all of the information and process the various possible scenarios. We felt we were in good hands but we could not be sure of the outcome. It was interesting to me that God would use a Hispanic man to help us and my son when we had helped many Hispanic people in our business and missions work. It actually gave me some comfort as it seemed to reinforce that God was involved. Being human, there were still many questions in my mind. Would things work out perfect? Would he survive but need further surgeries? Would he be in the small percentages that don't survive? With our faith we had never really contemplated nor were we prepared for him not surviving. But it's in those times when you feel the weakest, that God often sends a definitive sign of confirmation that he is taking care of things. And here it was again, right when we needed it. The last thing that Dr. Pubah said to us that night was, "tomorrow, The Lord will be in that operating room with us".

Seeking Comfort

Dr. Pubah's words had given me comfort. Comfort, I

knew, was only part of what I needed. I needed more, but what? I had previously decided that I would spend most of the night in the hospital chapel praying. I was determined to get alone with God and have a conversation with Him; a conversation full of questions and requests. It was spiritual warfare time and although God was on my side, I needed to have a wrestling match with Him in the form of prayer. It's a good thing that God is a God of mercy and grace and reads the intentions of our heart. My intentions were good but I believe I was mentally and physically exhausted. I prayed but I also drifted in and out of sleep. My home pastor had always said that everyone should get something out of church, even if it was a good nap; but even that was little relief. I really felt that I had failed in a simple task of prayer. It was a task much simpler than laying my life down for my son. I guess I was in good company as The Disciples had fallen asleep in the Garden of Gethsemane when praying with Jesus at a crucial time. It didn't make me feel much better about myself but the Bible knowledge I had learned was continually coming to mind and helping to carry the burden I felt.

A Date with Destiny

Morning had come and it was time to carry Skylar to

the surgery doors and hand him over to the surgery team. It was difficult to be facing the appointed time. I thought about the walk to execution on death row or the march to the gallows from long ago. Would it be worse to face your own appointed time or possibly that of a child? Although the statistical risk of death was low, the possibility has to be considered. I thought of how Abraham had to lay Isaac on the altar, in essence trusting God for the outcome. That is how I felt as I had no control over the situation but had to fully trust God for His perfect result. The hours ticked away in the waiting room as we waited. Occasionally we were given a report on his progress. Finally the answer came that the surgery was over and he was in recovery. The surgeon was able to make the heart repair using Skylar's own tissue. Because of the week delay in the surgery our five year old daughter came with friends to be with us. When our friends were there we were able to both be in the ICU unit with him. The doctors had told us that the after care of heart surgery was just as important as the surgery. Skylar not only had one nurse but two. As "chance" would have it a nurse was in training for ICU. This resulted in her also being assigned to him. When we first saw him it was a bit startling. Although it was evident that his color was already healthier looking from the heart functioning correctly, his physique still resembled that of a rubber chicken. On top of that there seemed to be tubes coming from or attached to every square inch of his body. Heart monitors, oxygen detectors, drain tubes, wires for an emergency pacemaker if needed, oxygen tube, feeding tube, and who knows what else were attached to this little body. There was even an IV that had been attached to his jugular vein. Is that even possible or safe I wondered? Then, the drugs started; Morphine and Versed injections every 15 minutes. I thought surely this is too much; so I asked. It was explained that due to a baby's small size and rapid metabolism, it was necessary to administer small doses at short intervals. Being proactive parents we stayed at his side and constantly touched him and spoke to him. Even the nurses explained that studies had shown that human touch and talk had a measured affect on patient recovery. This, we were told, was one of the reasons that their ICU had been opened up to allow family members being present around the clock. Only if another patient was in distress were we required to leave Skylar's side.

Hope

I don't remember a lot about the next couple of weeks of recovery time in the hospital. I remember our Pastor and other friends making the 500 plus mile trip to see us at the hospital. Their presence wasn't necessary but it was appreciated. I remember thinking how miraculous it was that modern medicine could do what it had done for Skylar. Had Skylar been born 10 or 20 years earlier, his heart defect would have been a death sentence. I thought of other families that had possibly faced this in years past. What emotions must they have felt knowing that their child would not live very long and there was nothing medical science could do? Or, going back even farther, I imagined what it would be like if Skylar's situation was faced in a time when medicine could not have detected a problem. Would it be harder watching your child get weaker and weaker, eventually succumbing to heart failure, knowing or not knowing what it was? At least we had the opportunity to have hope in modern medical science. Someone had told us about the old time Western Movie star Roy Rogers and his wife Dale Evans having a Down syndrome child. She was a beautiful little girl that only lived a short time. We read the book Dale Evans wrote about their child. It was written from the child's viewpoint as if talking to God. It was both a sad but uplifting true story of hope. I can't totally imagine the emotions that the Roger's were faced with. I can however understand their hope. Maybe we faced things on a slightly different level and time period. Maybe our child's date with death would be extended by successful surgery. Yet, just like all of us, we are destined to die and are on equal ground when it comes to needing hope. Thank God, I know where my Hope comes from.

With that hope and after having just come through the darkness; I could now finally see a glimmer of Light.

Skylar with the dark, tired, eyes; sits with Dad and his sister Alexis sometime before the surgery.

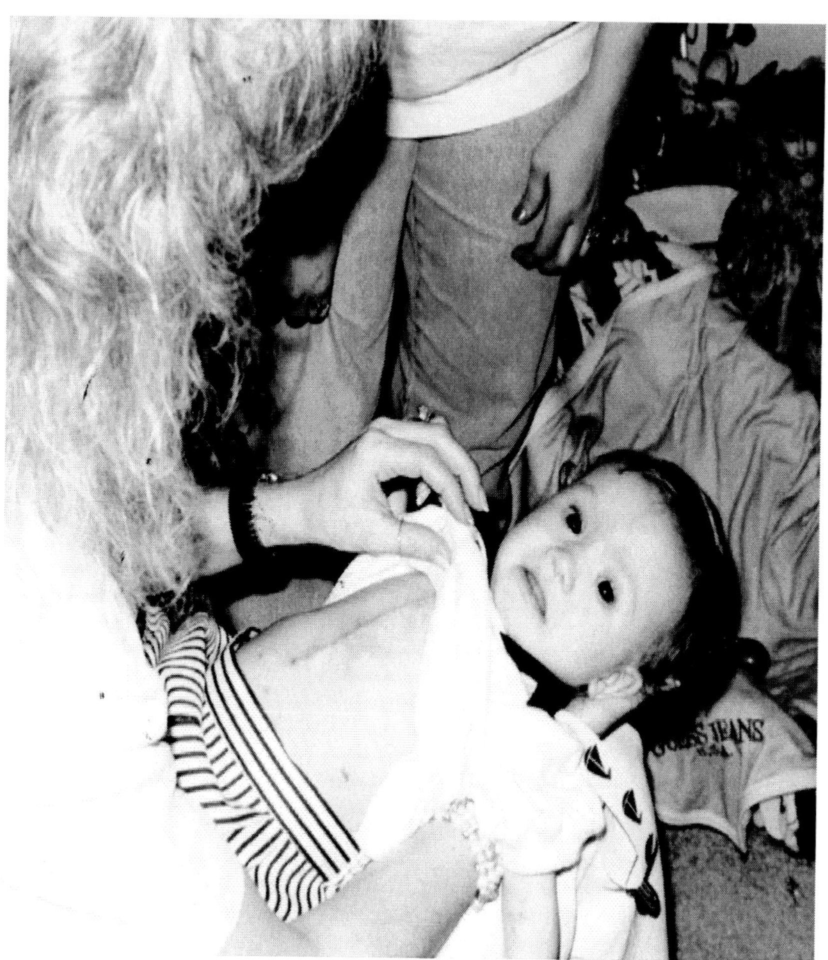

Skylar with his "zipper"; healthier and home.

Chapter 4

The Journey

A Journey is defined as traveling from one place
to another, usually taking a long time.
It is also described as a passage or
progress from one stage to another.

Beginning Again

Surgery was behind us and Sky was healthy now. We still had to make routine doctors visits. Visits to the pediatrician to monitor his growth and overall health, trips to the cardiologist to check the heart; all were important and necessary. There was also however, a renewed peace of mind. Sky's skin color was so much better. He was building strength and could eat better. His hometown cardiologist checked his heart by echocardiogram and said that Skylar's heart repair was the best he'd ever seen. Sky had come a long way from the rubber chicken physique he had for so many months. He was over a year old now and his health was improving. What do we do for him now? How do we help this child that is different than our other children? How do you find out or know what is best for his future? It's not that we always knew what to do or necessarily did the best for the other children we had raised and were raising. But, we did try hard. Having been "normal" children ourselves we at least had felt that we knew how his older siblings thought processes worked. With Sky, we really weren't sure what to do.

A Lot to Learn

And then it happened again, as if it was just random. While checking out a facility that could possibly work with him, mom meets a lady that is the parent of a Special Needs child. The lady says you need to take him to The Institute of Logopedics. My wife came home and told me about this "chance meeting". We had heard of the recommended facility but really didn't know much about it. I don't think I even knew what Logopedics meant. I didn't really like the Institute part and the thought of my son being institutionalized. It was my own paradigm of what I perceived institutes to be like. There were some positives though. We did know that it was a nationally recognized facility that worked someway with special needs children. We also knew that we had previously seen advertisements where their work was supported by a national television star. At the time we were having some assistance from another fine organization that did home visits. Wanting to learn more about what was available and how to help Skylar, we decided to check out "The Institute". Now when I say we, I really mean mom. Although she was and still is a gorgeous looking woman, one of the reasons I married my wife was I believed she was a remarkable mother. When we married she had two children and I saw her commitment to do what she felt was best for them. She was a physically small woman but when it came to those children she would protect them with all she had and was not bashful about it. I don't think I saw all of that before we were married but I must have sensed it somehow. I would have never dreamed that 11 years later that exact mothering ability would be so important for Skylar. I was busy running a business and trying to keep our heads above water financially. I was in on most of the major decisions in Skylar's life but it was mom that executed many of them. This she accomplished along with taking care of the daily needs of the three kids still at home. I probably never totally realized the load she carried until writing these words. So both of us went to "The Institute" for an initial meeting but it was mom that would take him to the vast majority of his later visits there. Also the facility moved to a brand new location and changed its name to Heartspring. This helped me a lot as it took away the thought of Sky going to an institute. Additionally, I didn't have to learn what Logopedics meant.

Therapy

I do really attribute a lot of Skylar's success in learning to the early intervention skills of Heartspring. It was there that we were told that you didn't want to read anything about Down syndrome that was over about 10 years old. My earlier paradigm was reinforced somewhat as they said that in the past it was thought most Down syndrome kids needed to be institutionalized. We were told that what experts thought about how Down syndrome diagnosed children learn and what they can accomplish had totally changed. We also learned that babies start learning from the use of motor skills. It had been discovered that the lack of muscle tone, which is common with Down syndrome children, causes delays in their learning. The poor muscle tone and a usually larger tongue also hamper their speech. They said it would be important for Skylar to do physical therapy. So, Skylar started going to Heartspring several times a week. At first they had him do what seemed like fairly simple things. The therapists would move his arms and legs to work his muscles. They also used a gloved finger to massage his mouth, gums, and tongue. This was to help his muscles, which would later be used for speech, to be stimulated and strengthened. As he got older his therapy would include other physical tests to help him crawl, stand, and walk. He later progressed to stair climbing and trying to pedal a tricycle. The physical therapy really seemed to be helping.

Trust the Experts?

It wasn't too long after Sky started going to Heartspring that I noticed that they were going to have a seminar on Down syndrome. They were bringing in an expert on Down syndrome to speak at the seminar. Her name was Dr. Lindsey Kummings. Well, I'm not the smartest guy nor profess to be. I had been to some seminars before on various topics. At most, I would think they were a waste of time and the person getting the most benefit out of it was the paid speaker. After all, they were the one taking my money and at the same time probably building some kind of a reputation as an "expert". I usually didn't think they were very smart or felt I learned very much. Perhaps it was my short attention span or maybe I was jealous at their being able to get paid to talk. Whatever the case, I decided to attend the seminar. I even paid the fee without reluctance. After all, I would surely learn something as I basically knew nothing about Down syndrome. The day came for the seminar and I went with an attentive and open mindset. Dr. Kummings spoke about how children with Down syndrome learn. I learned about the importance of repetitious and rhythmic learning. I learned that she devoted her career to studying and helping people with Down syndrome. I myself am certainly not one to limit what can be accomplished. Being an eternal optimist the proverbial glass is always more than half full to me. Maybe I see through rose-colored glasses and am optimistic to a fault, but so be it. Although I think that way, I was not as optimistic about how to help my son, most likely, due to lack of knowledge. At that seminar, things changed. I left that seminar with increased hopes and expectations based upon factual knowledge. I thought that Dr. Kummings truly was an expert. Everything she said made sense to me and seemed to coincide with what I had witnessed in watching Skylar. Her explanations placed in my mind the possibility of making a tangible plan for Skylar's learning. I had observed how Skylar acted and reacted to various stimuli, but I could not have explained how he thought. I knew in my mind and heart but needed an outline. Does that make sense? I told mom that there was not one thing Dr. Kummings said that I didn't agree with. For a non "status quo" kind of guy, this was a remarkable confession.

Fitting In

As Skylar grew I was amazed and fascinated by many things about him. Not only could he do the Chinese splits, but he could do them then lean forward and stand up. Chuck Norris and Jean-Claude Van Damme had nothing on Sky in the flexibility department. I'd think, special needs nothing, that's just special. I watched him accomplish many tasks and tried to figure out how he thought. In many ways it really wasn't much different than how every kid thinks and figures things out. One trait that did stand out was that he lined everything up. Sky would play with little toy cars and line them all up in a straight line. He would also get shoes out of the closet and line them up end to end; again always in a very straight line. Things that would slide across the floor easily he would line up and push; together like a train. If they got out of line he would stop and line them back up. I kept wondering if this was typical with Down syndrome kids. I did notice that he seemed to like rhythm and learned more easily if things were put to a rhythm. This was just as Dr. Kummings had said in the seminar. We were told that at a young age he would learn at a pace not too far behind other kids. He would not seem so different from other kids when young but, as he aged, the gap would become bigger. That's really not something that you want to believe about your child. We wanted to believe that our child had the capacity to accomplish anything as well as other kids. Our dream was to main stream educate Sky and have him do as many things as possible with regular kids.

You've Got to Try

A couple of the early things we would try on this journey were basketball and T-Ball. He loved basketball but the T-Ball season came first. The YMCA was very gracious in accepting Skylar for T-Ball. They told us that they had all kinds of kids on teams and would pick a team and coach suited to him and his needs. I started thinking this was easier than I thought. I had perceived him being shunned in sports, being preconceived as slow and a poor player. I had thought that I might have to be a strong advocate for him or he would not be accepted on a team. Well, T-Ball started and Skylar was allowed to play. Although I'm not embarrassed easily I secretly had a fear of possible embarrassment. I honestly don't know if that was fear of him being embarrassed or embarrassing myself. I hoped that I did not fear him being an embarrassment for me. God forgive me if I was. There really wasn't any problem with T-Ball so I guess my fears were unfounded. He played about as good as most of the kids and better than some. I maybe had to help him more than I had our other kids but it was okay. He wasn't overly accepted, but he wasn't shunned. After all how serious can a baseball league be that doesn't keep score. The number of runs scored and hits weren't counted but I still felt some were keeping score. Maybe it was paranoia but I felt that Sky was probably being rated by the other kids' parents. I imagine some were hoping he wouldn't be on their kid's team as they got older and the sports more competitive.

Try Again

With T-Ball being accomplished, I decided to have him try basketball. Sky loved basketball, just like his older brother. He was a good shot too, when playing on his small home goal. Maybe he could overcome any physical and mental disadvantages and compete at basketball. I was hoping he would surprise people. I knew that if it didn't work out he could try Special Olympics, but not for a few years until he was older. So we tried YMCA basketball. It was here that I had to face the fact that he just wouldn't be able to do some things as well as other kids. Although a basketball game between 4 and 5 year olds is a pretty chaotic scene, it is also played at a faster pace than T-Ball.

Where in T-Ball you pretty much stayed in one spot and might go after the ball if hit in your direction, in basketball, you are constantly going after the direction of the ball. I soon realized that Skylar just couldn't keep up with the quick back and forth movement. I also realized that he was more timid than the other kids when going after the ball. It didn't seem to be just his smaller size and lack of physical strength, but something else. Something more was evident than just a normal timidness that some kids have. This also went beyond being lackadaisical. All things considered, we quit basketball for the time being.

Try, Try Again

It would be much later through Special Olympics sports that I would realize that Sky's perceived weakness was nothing of the kind. It was actually a strength that many Special kids have. Maybe it's a spiritual strength. While many "Normal" people get caught up in a sometimes overly competitive and aggressive nature, I came to realize that most kids like Sky are not that way. They like to win and compete, but at the same time want everyone to win. There is something different about their kind of winning. It's something more profound that you can't totally put your finger on. It really is one of life's mysteries.

Now, I'm not saying that there shouldn't be competitive sports and a will to win. I played them myself and tried my best to win. After all, what would be the point if we didn't keep score? Just like everything in life, I think there probably needs to be a balance. Maybe kids like Sky help to balance things out for the overly competitive. Little did we know that Special Olympics would be a blessing for us. It would be a blessing that would touch all of our emotions and teach us a lot about Life.

Ouch

I was learning a lot about Sky and how he thought. I was also learning a lot about his physical strengths and weaknesses. I was also learning how others thought. There was one incident that stuck in my mind about how others think. It was at Silver Dollar City in Branson, Missouri when I first began to realize that Special kids are not always given to Special people. It may have been on the same trip where I forgot to strap him in the baby carrier and then carelessly flipped him out on the pavement. He fortunately wasn't hurt but it made me consider my standing in the world of parenting. At least this wasn't intentional like the scene I would soon witness. It happened at an evening concert at Silver Dollar City. We sat fairly high up in the open amphitheater. It was very crowded where we sat. We soon noticed that the family sitting in front of us had a Down syndrome son. He looked to be possibly early teens in age. The boy we figured out was with his mother, father, and sister. His sister was pretty nice to him. His mom seemed a little indifferent. Several times he came down in front of me to sit by his father. He tried to talk to his father and even hugged him. The father never acknowledged that he was there. Each time he would stare straight ahead and sit on his hands as if the boy was invisible. It would have been easier if someone had ripped my heart out and stomped on it. I can be a pretty stoic guy when it comes to showing emotion. My wife often says that I have one feeling, not feelings. None the less, this experience threw me into a storm of emotions. I was so angry that my blood boiled, making it very difficult to hold my tongue. At the same time my heart was broken with compassion and I was on the verge of tears. I couldn't completely know or understand that father's shunning of his child. As for me, I swore to myself that day that I would never show disregard for, be embarrassed of, or withhold affection from Sky. At the time I couldn't totally fathom the importance of this.

There's Always a Reason

As Sky grew up he developed a special bond with me, just like our daughter had experienced with mom. With our daughter I had sometimes felt slighted when she would almost always want mom and sometimes shunned me. I didn't understand that. I didn't think I had done wrong to her. Well, with Skylar, it was the total opposite. I was like his hero. He would stand waiting for me to come in the door from work. When I came in he would start with saying a slow breathless "my........my........my"; then finish with a loud, excited "MY DAD" as he ran into my arms. He needed Dad, just like the boy at Silver Dollar City needed his dad. I'm glad I had seen what I did with the other man and his son, but at the same time, I was still disgusted by it. I hurt for that boy. I've thought about him often and prayed his life got better. In some way I know God allowed me the experience so as to cement my will in how I would treat my son. It was just one more way that helped me realize that I was embarking on a journey. It would be a Journey of Life.

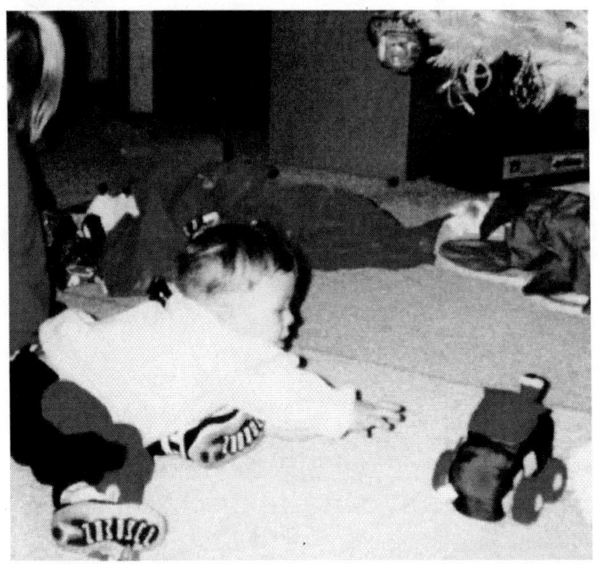

Sky learning to play

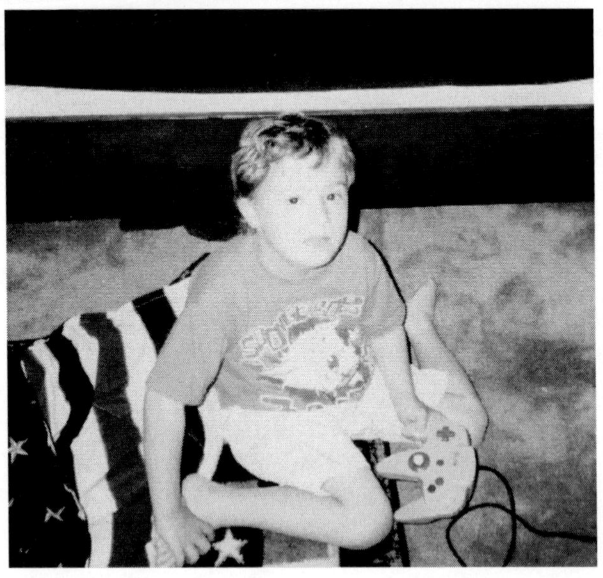

Sky with his bendable legs

Chapter 5

The Mind

Mind is defined as: one's intellect or the element that enables them to be aware of the world and their experiences, to think, and to feel; the faculty of consciousness and thought.

The Escape Artist

Most would probably think that Skylar and people like him lack intellect and have an underdeveloped mind. I propose that theirs may not be lacking but just different.

There are many incidents in Skylar's life and his traits that made me wonder how his mind worked. One thing that Skylar became proficient at was being an Escape Artist. We learned it pretty early on. Teachers would also learn it later when Skylar entered school as he would often just run out the door. I don't know who thought of putting the tape across the floor at the door as a boundary for him not to cross. It was maybe done as a last ditch effort or threat; like a line in the sand. Whatever it was it seemed to work and I wish I'd known of the tactic a lot sooner. It may have thwarted a couple of memorable escapes. The first happened in Washington D.C. at one of the money museums. Skylar was probably six or seven years old. He was still fairly small and he got tired walking. We would often have him rest in a small foldable stroller. We would always strap him in due to a couple of factors. One was because of the previously mentioned incident; where I hadn't strapped him in his carrier as a baby and dumped him on the pavement. The other was because he was prone to taking off. He had learned to open the stroller strap but it sometimes took him some effort. Strapping it gave us a little bit of a time buffer should he attempt an escape. All I remember is that we were at one of those portable photo booths waiting on our other kids. Suddenly, someone asked where Skylar was. I said he's in the stroller while simultaneously looking and realizing; he wasn't in the stroller. As pre-panic concern for where he was set in, I started looking around for him. I realized he wasn't nearby or in the photo booth. I then immediately said "I'll look outside, you guys look inside". I ran outside and just as I got out the door, a Police Officer that worked at the museum was standing there. He had hold of Sky's hand and was bringing him back in. What a relief it was that this officer had been observant and diligent in his duty. He had seen Sky come out the door and realized he probably needed detained. He wasn't a true criminal or terrorist but to me he kind of was. His unauthorized escape from confinement had definitely terrorized me. He had been apprehended by an officer of the law. I then thought I ought to count my blessings because I was most likely the bigger criminal based upon my lack of properly watching him. In our ever increasing litigious society my bad parenting coupled with about losing my child is probably a crime somewhere. I hope that in admitting to this I am past any statute of limitations. In my defense I would argue that it really happened fast. He must have been practicing his escape by secretly manipulating that latch. I mean I'd never seen him unlatch it as quick as he evidently did. I should have changed his name to Houdini.

Where's Sky?

Another incident happened at a hotel in Arkansas. I'm going to blame this on someone else too. But it's not Sky this time. It's his siblings. I guess you could say that I'm ultimately responsible for everything that happens in my family. I'll accept that, but it is tempting to pass the buck, so to speak, by claiming lack of responsibility. I like to say, if asked to be in charge of something, that "I'll be irresponsible for that". That could sum up a majority of my parenting. If you admit you'll be irresponsible, it really takes the pressure off in regard to meeting others' expectations. So, back to the story; we were in this hotel. The wife and I were up early and because our room was adjacent to the breakfast area, we decided to get coffee together. Now normally one of us would get the coffee while the other stayed in the room with the kids. Since Sky's brother and sister were getting a little older and his brother was a teenager, we thought surely we could leave him asleep in the room with them for a few minutes. Boy, were we wrong. We had our coffee and returned to the room after only being gone about 10 minutes. When we opened the door we saw the kids still asleep. But, where was Sky? He wasn't in the bed. He wasn't in the bathroom. That sick feeling that you get in the pit of your stomach came over me. While I tried to be calm on the exterior and start a logical search, I was churning with emotion on the inside. We were in a big multi-story hotel. Sky could have gone anywhere. Also he was so trusting of people, anything could have happened. This was one of those moments that can change lives forever. All kinds of things run through your mind from, how could I have been so stupid, to what if my special child that God entrusted to me is gone forever? A search had to be started. First my wife told the front desk. Hopefully one of the hotel staff had seen him. Our son started looking on the first floor. My wife and daughter went outside to search.

These were the most logical places to look. I mean surely he wouldn't have gone on an elevator. For some unknown reason, I thought I should check the other floors. So that is the direction I went. Probably only 5 minutes or less had elapsed but it seemed like hours. I got on the elevator and decided to go systematically floor by floor and ask anyone I saw if they had seen him. Again for some unknown reason I decided to go to the fourth floor first and work my way down. I came off the elevator, all the while thinking that he was gone for good. To have that thought was completely out of character as I am typically, if anything, overly optimistic. I don't tend to get rattled easily, but I was rattled. I turned the corner to the first hall. I then turned another corner. It is still many years later embedded in my mind that I went left then right in my journey. I rounded the second corner and there he was; sitting on the floor. A flood of warmth spread through my body as the stress started to lift. I scooped him up and held him tight. I don't remember what I said but I know in my heart and spirit I was apologizing to him and God. Of course I immediately called mom and said "I've got him". If I was feeling the emotions of his loss so deeply, I can't imagine what his mother was feeling. I truly believe that mothers are predestined to have the deepest emotional bonds with their children in a way that fathers usually can't understand. This may have been the one time when I thought I was brought to the verge of understanding that deep mother/child bond.

It is also a moment like this when I believe that not just the mind, but the heart also, is somehow emotionally connected. From that day forward, I vowed to better watch my kids. I hope I did, although life fatigue and sometimes laziness can make one fall short in upholding that vow. I mean children are a precious gift that should be guarded at all times as our most valuable possession. After all they are our earthly legacy of immortality. Perhaps Sky's skill of escape and my willingness to tell of my ineptness in properly watching him will benefit someone. Our stories of loss turned out positive. I pray that others don't ever have the experience. Sky' escaping was just one example of where the term "Where's Sky?" would become a common phrase in our family. Some would be scary while others would end up comical. Whatever the case "Where's Sky?" would always result in something memorable.

School Daze

Skylar was growing more every day, although slowly. Heartspring had helped him immensely but it became time for him to gain more formal learning. Our desire was for him to follow in his older siblings footsteps and attend the Christian preschool and grade school that they attended. When it came time for preschool my wife decided to put Skylar in a church preschool that specialized in preschool only. I was okay with that as I thought the reasoning was that they did preschool only and might be better at it. I eventually asked her one day why she hadn't placed him in the other school. She said it was because they wouldn't take him. She reminded me that our preferred school choice required kids to pass an entrance exam to be accepted. I usually deferred to my wife on matters of daily things with the kids, as she was a stay at home mom. It was her primary job to take care of the kid's daily schedules and care. Thankfully, this was something she excelled at. Sky fit in pretty good at preschool. He could mostly do what the other kids could. I thought maybe the learning gap between him and the "normal" kids wouldn't be as great as we had been warned about.

Unexpected Help

It then became time to move on to Kindergarten. Again, due to our preferred school's entrance test requirements, we decided to try public school. It wasn't that we were opposed to public school; it's just that we preferred Christian school. After all, both of us were products of public school. I remember having some really fine teachers and we have multiple friends that are great teachers in the public school system. So,

Skylar began Kindergarten at the public school. His teacher was Miss Paula. Miss Paula seemed like a very caring individual. This would later prove to be a big understatement. School was still a learning process for us. We knew nothing about Special Education or what Sky's capabilities were. As time went on we learned more about both his teacher and about how Special Education works. This time in Public School would later prove to be very helpful in Sky's future education. Sometime during his time in Kindergarten, I again asked my wife about him going to the Christian School. I saw no reason why a "Christian" school would not be accepting of all kids. I began to think that maybe Skylar would be good for the school. Again my wife reminded me of the entrance requirements, but she was not opposed to trying. We decided to apply to the Christian school. During the process we were required to meet with a group of the educators. Knowing our hearts for trying to do the best for Skylar, teacher Paula said she would go with us and speak on his behalf. This was totally unexpected, but deeply appreciated. Again, I felt that God had placed someone specifically in Skylar's life at a particular time and for a specific purpose.

It Ain't Over 'til It's Over

Well, I thought the meeting went pretty well. Teacher Paula had been a great advocate for Skylar. He would still be required to take the entrance test but I felt that it was understood that he most likely wouldn't be able to pass it. Although we found out that the school had never accepted a kid with known learning disabilities, we decided to proceed. Well, sure enough, Sky didn't pass the test. It was left to one of the administrators to tell us that Skylar wasn't accepted. The decision was mostly made, I believe, by a staff committee. It was emphasized that everyone wanted to help Skylar but they felt the school was not equipped or staffed to properly educate him. I personally thought the school was as prepared or equipped as it ever would be. I asked if there was some kind of an appeal process to the board of the school. We were told that we could make a formal appeal and meet with the church board that oversaw the school. The meeting was scheduled for an evening. While preparing for the meeting at home, I got out a framed picture of Skylar. Mom asked me what I was doing. I said, I'm taking this to the meeting. She questioned whether that would be proper or if it would go over well. I said that I wanted them to see him as a real person. After all, it is commonly stated, a picture is worth a thousand words. Though we couldn't take him there in person it would, in a sense, be a face to face meeting. I believed that it was a lot harder for human beings to deny something to another human face to face, than in writing or in their absence. I was counting on that to be true. All we could do at the meeting was to present our case and show our deep desire that Skylar be given the same education quality as our other children had received at the school. During the meeting, I explained to the board that we felt that the school was more prepared to help Skylar in the ways we wanted him to be educated than the public schools would ever be. Again, this was nothing against the public schools. We just felt that the heart of the Christian teachers, many that we already knew, would provide the overall nurturing environment that we felt would benefit Skylar the most. I also stated that I thought Skylar would possibly be as good for the school as the school would be for him. Though I'm not the most emotional guy, at that meeting it was hard to hold back tears. I felt that it was hard for the men of the board also. We could feel the desire in their hearts to help Skylar. It would be a few days before we would know the outcome of the board's vote. We were hopeful that they would see things our way but not confident of that. We were later notified by the school that the board had decided to accept Skylar but there would be certain requirements. It was an apprehensive victory but, we perceived, a victory none the less.

Worth The Cost

We were soon called in to meet with the Headmaster of the school. We knew him as a very compassionate and gracious man. It was at this meeting that we were made aware of the school's requirements. Skylar would be accepted but we would have to provide or pay for a full time paraprofessional to assist him. The school had always wanted to help learning disabled kids but hadn't felt prepared. Skylar was the first student to have known learning disabilities to ever be accepted there. I was so overjoyed that I probably didn't totally figure the cost. I just said that I didn't care what it took; I was willing to work 16 hour days if needed to cover the cost. In my heart I was trusting God to provide the finances. In my mind I was maybe not so sure. After all, we were only a few years past the hardest financial time of our lives and were rebuilding our business. I know that nothing is impossible with God. God however, often requires something from us in His plan. Our part can often be difficult. It started to sink in that we would be facing school tuition for three kids plus the cost of a paraprofessional. The paraprofessional cost would be as much as the three tuitions combined.

The Unexpected Happens

Mom on the other hand had a different concern about schooling than the cost. Her main focus was on how we would find the right helper for Skylar. The school would assist us in finding someone, but the burden was also on us. Again, God stepped in to provide an answer. It was, as is often like Him, a totally unexpected answer. One day the wife of the school's assistant headmaster contacted us. Her husband had been the one that initially had to turn down our request for Skylar to attend the school. She told us that she had been praying for a paraprofessional to help Skylar. We thought that she must have someone in mind. She went on to explain that while praying, God spoke to her and said, "Why can't you be his paraprofessional?" What an unexpected answer. So that's what we did. Maybe God did it just as much for her as for Skylar and us. Sky would only have this helper for one year, but over the years God would provide an amazing string of people to help him. He would have overqualified people step forward over and over to be his paraprofessional. Not for the relatively small sum of money, but out of compassion. They really were added teachers to the ones he had for each grade or class. He was different but the kids loved him. Certain ones would befriend him and eat lunch with him every day. One particular lady that helped him for several years when he got older, I always in my mind compared to Annie Sullivan. Many of us know Annie Sullivan as the teacher who helped a deaf and blind Helen Keller. Ms. Sullivan was helping a child that in her day was considered deaf, DUMB, and blind. Her results were astonishing to say the least. Our "Annie Sullivan" was with Skylar multiple years during his older, more educable, years. I believe she learned how he thought. This really helped him in his learning. Skylar always progressed beyond what we thought he could accomplish. He learned the alphabet, he learned to read, and he learned to add, subtract and even multiply. The one on one teaching that the school required was actually a blessing in disguise as it resulted in more focused teaching; which is what he needed. We couldn't have done it in a home school setting with him or any of our kids. We are hard working and fairly intelligent enough, but probably not structured enough to provide quality home schooling. If we'd have tried it, we were at least smart enough to know, the result would have been dumb kids. We would have been the opposite of Annie Sullivan. We would have taken naturally smart kids and made them dumb. I say this somewhat tongue-in-cheek but it is true. We would not have been good at schooling our kids, Skylar included. Our children's achievements have been largely from their own efforts and we believe Divine Intervention. Nonetheless, we did our part and their achievements were expected. In Skylar's case the results were totally unexpected.

It Just Gets Better

Sometimes Sky's ability to learn would totally amaze me. He had been taking a class, which we paid extra for, called Semple Math. It was fairly costly. It was costly enough that I questioned its value. Finally I decided to sit in on a session. It was done in a library office with a particular teacher. During the class she wrote some long numbers on the board. She then told Skylar to add up the five or six 9 digit numbers. She called the groups of numbers parents and kids. Well sure enough, Sky added the numbers up correctly at the bottom of the board. I was pretty amazed by that but still thought it wasn't super difficult math. Then the teacher told Sky to read the number. Surprisingly to me he read off the number that was in the tens of billions. I think he was in about 6th grade. I was totally amazed. I know lots and lots of grown, so called normal, people that couldn't have done that. Needless to say, I left there a little embarrassed that I ever questioned the cost of Semple Math. I'd seen enough and never ventured back.

What's Next?

Sky went on to graduate from that school when he finished the eighth grade. It was quite an accomplishment that he was very proud of. It would be a difficult time for us to have to leave that school. It only went through eighth grade. The Christian high school that our other kids had attended really didn't have programs for him. It looked like we would probably venture back to public school. The kids that had grown to love him the last nine years would mostly be going to the Christian school. It was sad that he'd probably lose touch with them, but such is life. Times change for everyone and you sometimes have to move forward and let go of some of the past. He'd make new friends. They may be mostly special education kids, but maybe it was time for that. And maybe, just maybe, he would bring something to them.

Life Can Be a Party

And Sky did bring something to them and likewise, them to him. His high school years brought something to us too. A highlight of the year for me was when the Special Ed classes came to our house for a cookout and swim party. Sometimes we would have as many as forty kids there along with various teachers. It was both a humbling and exciting time. There were kids with all kinds of different needs; some were in wheelchairs, a few with Down syndrome, many with Autistics, some verbal, others non-verbal, those that were higher functioning and several lower functioning. Each had their own challenges combined with a unique personality. I realized that most of the teachers just loved them as they were. It was amazing how they could relate to all of the kids and communicate with them. There were always some hi-jinks going on too. It wasn't unlike any other party for High School kids in that regard. Most were just harmless things that occurred in attempts to have fun. A close eye was kept on the kids with a limited number allowed in the pool at one time. We did have a girl run off in the adjacent field and have to be chased down by the teachers. Another time things could have turned out bad when we couldn't find a couple of kids. It was time for everyone to leave and they wanted a group picture. This is when we couldn't find two of the kids. One of course was Skylar. Then I heard a loud familiar noise out in the field. Earlier Sky's older brother had been giving some kids rides in Skylar's miniature gas powered dune buggy. I thought he had finished that earlier and put it away. Then I saw the dune buggy with two kids in it flying by; the driver, Skylar of course. He had one of his friends with Down syndrome riding with him. They were going really fast. To cap it off, they didn't have helmets on. I had to do something, and quick. Well I did get them stopped. I needed to reprimand Skylar but I didn't want to be too harsh in front of the others. Plus, they both had huge grins on their faces. They were having a blast. Nevertheless, Skylar needed talked to. I told him he shouldn't have been driving without permission. I then asked him why they didn't have their helmets on. He said they did. I said, "No you didn't". Sky said, "They are right there"; as he pointed to the helmets sitting on the rack right behind the dune buggy seats. Well he was right. They did have them on, on the dune buggy, just not on their heads. I still was fairly stern with him about how that wasn't smart and they could have been hurt very badly. My reprimand of Skylar however was nothing compared to what the other kid got. The other kid had Down syndrome and also had a hearing disability. Although he could hear and understand a little, he also had a particular teacher that helped communicate with him by using sign language. Let's just say, he got THE SIGN LANGUAGE. I don't know what she said but her hands were moving so fast it sounded loud to me. I guessed that's how you shout in sign language. I know it wasn't, but I always referred to it as the only time I ever saw someone get cussed out in sign language. Excluding of course a few common gestures I've seen and maybe used. She didn't use any of those gestures and was I'm sure yelling in complete visual sentences. I felt bad for the kid but, boy, it was impressive.

Some people would tell me that maybe we shouldn't have the parties due to chances of liability if an accident occurred. I did think about that. I think the school maybe had some type of waivers signed but I never asked about it. When I saw the smiles on those kids faces it made life okay for me. From the ones in the pool with squirt guns, to the ones thrilled with the hamburgers, to even one immobile kid that would crawl to the refrigerator and help himself to yogurt, which he loved; this annual event would bring tears to my eyes and make me smile. These kids were really teaching me something and giving me a sense of value. Maybe, just maybe God was pleased and providing me a sense of purpose.

I've heard it said that a mind is a terrible thing to waste. Many with a lot do waste what they have been blessed with. I assure you that though we may not always see it, these, often considered to have the least, use their minds and can positively affect our minds in supernatural ways.

Sky is learning to read. I'm not sure why he's in a suit; maybe practicing for his future speaking engagement.

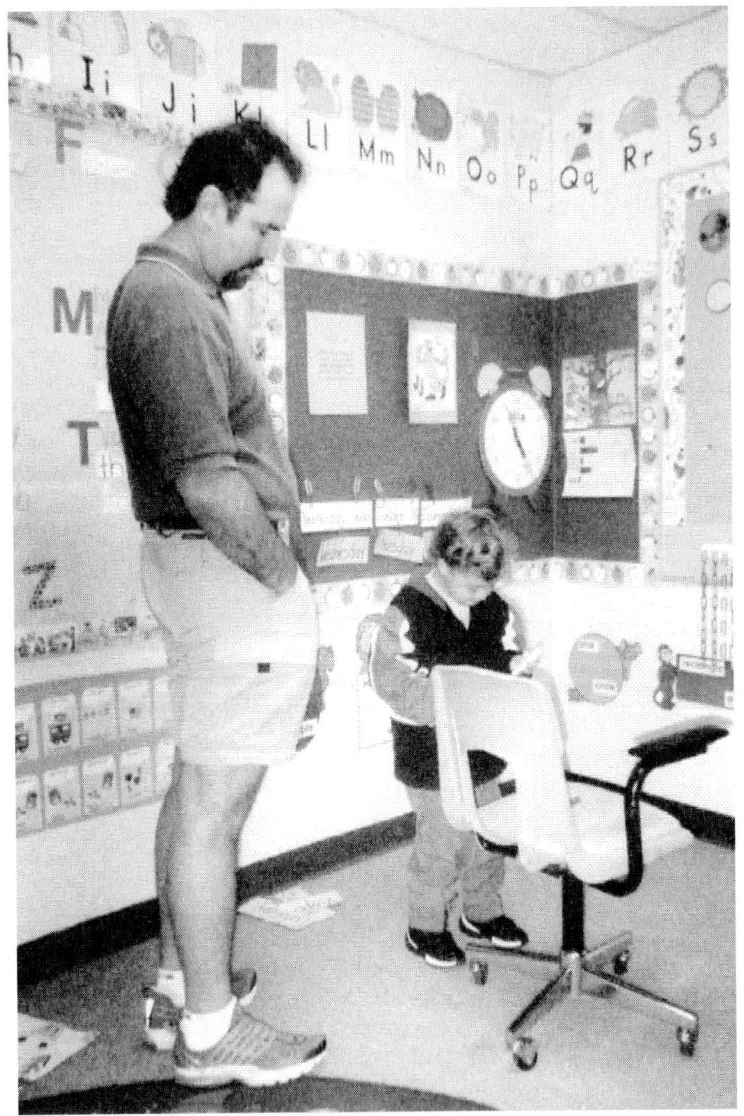

This is about the age Sky blew my mind in Semple Math by reading a number in the Billions.

Chapter 6

The Spirit

Spirit is defined as: the nonphysical part of a person that is the seat of emotions and character; the soul.

Quite a Character

Boy, would we learn what a character this kid could be. He had quite the spiritual soul, but more about that later. Sky, simply put, could make you laugh. It wasn't always intentional but we were always laughing with him; even, when we were laughing at him. We've probably all laughed at folks in special education at one time or another. I mean, they can really be funny. It took Skylar, and being around others like him, that we learned its okay to laugh at them. Not to make fun of them in a cruel way about a physical or social difference. That's not cool. You can though laugh at things they say and do just like you might anyone else. Your heart knows how you mean things. You may be laughing at a particular action but you're actually laughing with them. They do so with each other and, believe me, they know the difference. I believe a lot of people with special needs have an acute sixth sense toward things of the spirit. This includes reading laughter and its intention. It also includes sensing other human characteristics. For instance, it was rare for Skylar not to like someone. I mean he could talk to, hug, and when younger, kiss some of the people that many would consider the least desirable. We figured out that if Skylar didn't like someone, we too should be wary of them. We didn't see this often though. Most generally Skylar was happy, upbeat, and accepting of everyone. He could totally accept you and simultaneously make you the subject of his mischievous comments. Accidentally, or on purpose, he could come up with some of the most memorable and classic lines of speech.

The Urinal

One of his most memorable lines for me would be a little off color, so if you easily find things offensive, particularly male bathroom humor, turn the page now. You may regret it and suffer the suspense though, should you decide to skip ahead. The story began simple and innocent enough. One of Skylar's favorite places to eat was a major Mexican food restaurant chain. It was funny enough that the meal he always ordered was chicken strips, but he did love chips and salsa too. He was probably about 10 years old when the incident happened. Sky and I went to the bathroom together. There were two urinals side by side. One was short for kids and one taller. Well, the shorter urinal was being used by a guy that was probably in his late twenties in age. Although he'd probably have to stand on his tiptoes, Sky goes to the tall urinal. That relegates me to the adjoining stall. Now, Sky's a friendly fellow and it would not be a surprise for him to talk to someone at the urinal. I couldn't see him but I did hear him. He was probably looking over at the guy when he said those four simple words, "Mine's bigger than yours". I remember my eyes opened wide when I heard him and time seemed to stand still. Then, the guy next to him let out a hysterical laugh. I think he said, "that's classic". Well, it was classic. I think Sky meant his urinal was bigger, but we'll never know and I'm sure not going to ask.

Skyisms

Sky had a lot of memorable lines over the years. Where they came from was sometimes puzzling. Just like our other kids, we would sometimes later find out it came from a TV show or movie. Sky's timing in delivering comedic lines was extraordinary. Just like an accomplished comedian that sets up the right scenario to deliver the punch line, Sky could somehow accomplish the same thing. I couldn't figure out how though. Maybe accidental, maybe otherworldly, or maybe it was just a gift he had. Some things didn't go over too well. When he would open and close his hand quickly resembling a bird beak flapping and say "this is what you're doing", then close it and say "this is what I want you to do"; it was funny. When he did it to his mother, it wasn't quite as funny. He would always use it at appropriate times, although some might think inappropriate. I would later figure out he got this from a TV show. Other comments just came from him. Often the comments came at someone's expense. Like the time he was riding with his sister and her husband. I wasn't with them but the story relayed to me was classic Skylar. His brother-in-law had a few tattoos, mostly inconspicuous. Sky must have been noticing them and thinking about them. His comment would reflect that he probably wasn't admiring them. I guess he'd thought about it as long as he could so he spoke, "what happened, did you get all drunked up and get some tattoos?" Sky had a great relationship with his brother-in-law but he just called it like he saw it. His brother-in-law didn't even drink so I don't know how he related tattoos to drinking. I'm not sure it was related in this instance or in many others, but in some ways, he'd probably once again hit the nail on the head. I remember an incident where he was at basketball practice with some other Special Olympians. I noticed Sky talking to an older girl. She had one eye squinted and was kind of glaring at him. I wasn't sure what she was saying but it looked like she wasn't too happy with him. Now Sky's ornery, in a usually good way, so I thought he could have been teasing her. Still she was older and I wanted to make sure he was okay and the situation didn't escalate. When he came to the sidelines I asked him what was going on. He of course said he wasn't doing anything to her. I said well what was saying to you. Then he delivered another classic Sky answer, "I don't know, the one-eyed lady, she got slobbers all over her mouth". "She's not thinking straight." I probably shouldn't have laughed inwardly or outwardly like I'm sure I did. His remark sounded like something any other kid might say. Then when I looked closer, I realized he was right about the slobber. One side of me feels kind of bad for my thinking his comment funny. The other side of me felt even worse for thinking that if the guy with Down syndrome thinks you're not thinking straight; you might really have problems.

The depth of Sky's humor and where it came from was often baffling. It may have sometimes been accidental but I think it was most often intentional. When he was an early teen, I overheard a conversation he was having with his older brother Colt. I don't remember the exact subject but whatever it was that Sky was trying to explain; Colt wasn't getting it. It could have been Sky's speech or some abstract thought process in explaining it that hampered his, eight years older, brother from understanding. Regardless of the subject or reasoning, another classic "Skyism" was delivered when he said "it's complicated Colt, okay, it's complicated". Evidently Sky was fed up with Colt not understanding what he was telling him and must have figured Colt wasn't intelligent enough to get it. Sky learned humor from others also; so as he got older, like with all kids, we had to be more careful of what we said. I was the worst at this, or the best, depending on how you look at it.

The Lips

Skylar was totally special in his humor. He was a special person delivering special lines to describe special situations; like how he described his first kiss of a girlfriend. He came home from a birthday party at a Pizza Hut and as he often did, had a smirk on his face. That smirk typically meant something special had happened that he was itching to tell. Now it seems most Down syndrome folks are brutally honest and just blurt out the truth. Skylar is no different but in some situations he would intentionally hold back and want someone to ask. He may prompt you eventually by saying "tell me", as he often used the words tell and ask opposite of their normal use. If family saw the smirk, one of us would usually prompt him by just saying "what?" Well someone in this situation did just that. What was Skylar's reply? "I went LIP to LIP. He then went into detail about how he started his moves resulting in the ultimate deed in the foyer, where he strategically had maneuvered to. This relationship didn't last too much longer and I'm not sure he went LIP to LIP with that girl again. I think that he had reached his goal and scored. So, like many young males, he was ready to move on.

Not Pretty Good

Skylar came up with a lot of other unique sayings. Many of his sayings we adopted as we thought they pretty much summed up certain life situations in the simplest of terms. One that he used a lot was when something hadn't gone well or he didn't like something. We'd ask something like, how'd that go for you Sky?; His common reply; "not pretty good". He wasn't dejected or sad but summed up the situation in a very simple but what seemed an optimistic way. It was like it hadn't gone well but wasn't a big deal and almost comical. I think "not pretty good" became a tag line that we could use in our family to comment on situations that hadn't gone so well. It could help us to shrug them off. Skylar's humor could actually reach deep into your soul and lift you up. It could almost be healing if you really contemplated some of his comments. The Bible says that laughter is like a good medicine. It also, in my belief, is a valuable manuscript for living a happy and fulfilling life; if you contemplate its words. I often thought that many of Sky's comments, even the comical ones, tapped into spiritual truths. All you had to do was think about it and search your soul just like a Biblical Truth. If you're having a bad day and just think of it as "not pretty good", I think it brings it into perspective as maybe not being so bad.

Number Two

Sky used a lot of other sayings and some other memorable tag lines; like a long "noooooo", (pronounced like new) when he wanted to emphasis a negative answer. Another was "I hate two". I think he only used the latter a few times. The first occurred when we were on a vacation with most of our family. Sky was taking steroids to help his Crohn's disease. We were going to Disney World and because there were so many of us we decided to pack sandwiches (that plan of course lasted only about one day). The steroids would clear up the Crohn's flair ups but could only be given for a few weeks. A couple of the side effects were they made him really hungry and sometimes gave him "Moon Face". This was a kind of puffing under the chin and rounding of the face. This time it seemed both his hunger and "Moon Face" were greater. Although he was normally fairly thin and not a big eater, at one lunch he ate 23 chicken nuggets and a piece of lemon pie. Of course that is probably bad parenting but I think because we had a lot of family there and his moving to different tables, we didn't realize it right away. Sky noticed his face too as he'd look in a mirror and say "I'm all blowed up". Of course once he knew it got a laugh, he would periodically say it at random times. Anyway, back to the sandwiches. Someone was making the sandwiches for him for the day. Sky had gotten to wanting just butter sandwiches. That's right; two pieces of bread with butter in between. Kind of like I heard the Blues Brothers song about a Wish Sandwich; two pieces of bread and you wish you had some meat. Again, I'll get back to the story. Well, mom is thin and she saw Sky puffing up and eating too much. So, she decided to limit his intake. He would have a limited number of sandwiches for lunch. Normally, if not on steroids, he would eat half a sandwich or one at the most. After some negotiation, mom had the last word and said, "Okay, you can have two sandwiches". But mom didn't get the last word, Sky did. "I hate two", he said. The number two would never be the same for our family. Occasionally it would come up in conversation and Sky would cease the moment to repeat his line. Of course many of us would do the same thing. For our family, remembering the number two was imbedded in our minds better than it ever could have been by The Count, some other Sesame Street Character, or a classroom. And, like many of the things in life, there was something else that we could blame, or maybe thank. We later found that when converting the steroid dosage unit of measure for the droppers used on a prescription refill; the pharmacy made a mistake. Sky had been getting a double dose. As is often the case in Life, a choice had to be made. Do we blame them or forgive them? We all make mistakes I thought and we all need a little grace at times. After all, there were no lasting effects or a permanent Moon Face. Without the error the number two may have remained just an insignificant number to us. Like many of Sky's comments, "I hate two", would provide continued smiles for years to come. I chose to forgive them; better yet thank them.

Winning the Contest (Where's Sky again)

Have you ever been on a cruise ship? It can be a pretty fun and fairly low cost vacation. If you are afraid of water or get seasick easily it may not be for you. If you don't want to be in close proximity to a lot of strangers from all walks of life, it's probably not for you either. The pool area on some can get a little wild too, particularly if there is a lot of alcohol flowing. Some might say it can be a little vulgar at times. That being said there is usually other areas on the ship that you can go to find solace or a different atmosphere. That being the truth, I wonder why we were by the pool in the first place. This was going to be a memorable trip for a couple of reasons. One involved all of us. Both involved Sky. The latter incident resulted in Skylar almost getting smashed by a huge rolling video game that came loose from the wall. This was caused by the ship violently leaning in calm seas due to swerving to miss something in the water. If Sky wouldn't have kept playing the game as it rolled back toward him, he wouldn't have been in as much peril. Neither would I have had to grab his arm, kick the machine, and jerk him out of the way. It was especially eventful also to my grandson that got lodged in a big pool slide and my son whose chair slid across the pool deck as half of the water spilled out of the pool. All of the incidents were due to the list of the ship. Our family was all okay and the rest of the trip was uneventful. In the scheme of life's ups and downs the previous parts of the trip balanced out the latter potential tragedy. I guess for once it was a good thing I was actually keeping a close eye on Sky because in most instances I wasn't always doing so well. Unlike the latter incident involving Sky, in the first incident I was as usual not watching him close enough. Like I'd said earlier we were up by the pool. There was music and a few contests going on that we tried to steer clear of. Most were for adults and it appeared that entering the contests was predicated by various degrees of intoxication. We were just sitting by the pool and letting the kids swim while staying what we thought was a safe distance from the dancing and stage area. Suddenly I got that sixth sense feeling of having a missing kid. I don't know if it was actually that or the sound of the deejay's voice that made me say it again, "WHERE'S SKY?" All I know is I heard the microphones deejay say something like, what are you doing up here, this is for adults. With either an innate parental response or a Pavlov's Dog type response from knowing Sky; I headed toward the stage. There he was on stage with a bunch of middle aged, or worse, my aged, people. They were starting a contest so I started to work my way through the crowd to get him and maybe save some embarrassment. Then I heard the deejay say, "Okay you can stay". I then stood dumbfounded as I watched a bunch of guys that were at least as gross and hairy as me start to gyrate one at a time in front of a line of women. I'm not sure you could call it dancing and if sober, would definitely call it embarrassing. There was however, one dancer that was not inebriated nor did he have body hair. He was also the youngest. He was also my son. As usual, Sky brought down the house. He was of course not embarrassed and was definitely the best dancer. Yes he gyrated and did similar vulgar moves in close proximity to each of the middle-aged women, just as the other contestants had. Because the contest was for adults he wasn't given a participation trophy as his entourage was. He was however so good that after the contest a very gracious man who was one of the least inebriated, gave Sky his trophy. And that's how Sky won the contest. The contest was pretty early in the trip so we would see Sky repeatedly throughout the week on video monitors around the ship as they showed cruise highlights. Oh, I forgot to tell you the contests name:

The Hairy Chested Man Contest.

The Chicken Incident

Some of Sky's humorous lines came out of difficult or near tragic occurrences. I wasn't with him and his mother when a near tragedy occurred. Skylar had been eating food from one of his favorite places. As he often did he was stuffing in the chicken nuggets while mom drove. Suddenly he began choking. Mom figured out that this wasn't a minor situation and he had food lodged in his throat. As quickly as possible she stopped and got him out of the car beside the road and tried to dislodge the food. It was to no avail so she decided to dial 911 for help. She also prayed. As was often the case in Skylar's life, someone showed up when he most needed it. Not just anyone, but a doctor. It was not one of Sky's doctors but the father of some kids that Sky's older siblings had gone to school with. The doctor and his son had just happened to see Skylar by the side of the road and knew something was wrong. Not only did the doctor and his son try to help Skylar physically, they furthermore helped him and his mother emotionally. The doctor held Skylar's hand and talked to him in a soothing manner to calm him down. His presence and care were reassuring to both mom and Skylar. Skylar calmed down but then shortly began coughing. This dislodged the chicken. He had been spared of needing the paramedics. As he would tell the story, he evidently was spared by the chicken too. If you asked Sky what happened he said "I got choked by a chicken". Being fairly advanced in years I would recall vivid images in my mind of the San Diego Chicken from years past. The famous costumed mascot would often grab fans during his baseball game antics; I believe even sometimes pretending to choke them. Of course many male friends of mine would raise an eyebrow when Sky said he got choked by a chicken. I don't want to repeat or explain what they were thinking. Just suffice it to say that it could have fit into the late comedian George Carlin's skit about what you could and couldn't say on television.

Watch Your Language

Every decent parent is concerned about the language their children use. We tend to become more concerned as they get older and know the difference between appropriate and inappropriate language. One of our greatest fears is that they will pick up the use of inappropriate words at school; words that they also might learn in most good homes if the dad smacks his finger with a hammer or the mom burns her hand on the stove. I guess in today's world it could just as easily be vice versa. Skylar didn't seem to pick up the use of any profane words at home or anywhere else throughout his younger years. When he entered high school our concerns, like many parents, increased in regard to learning and or repeating bad language. It was bad enough that we had not been able to break him of using his middle finger to point, instead of his index finger. I swear this wasn't a hereditary trait or learned at home. Well, high school seemed to be going pretty good and Skylar didn't appear to be learning any profane words. In fact it seemed like his mind almost worked in the opposite way, or blocked things out entirely. If one of the words that most tend to consider less offensive on the cussing scale was used unexpectedly in a movie or on television; Skylar seemed to ignore it. It was as if he never heard the word. I happily assumed that the same thing was happening at school or other times when he wasn't with us. That was what I hoped anyway until that fateful day when “it happened”. Skylar came home from school one day and with a serious look on his face said he had something to tell us. My assumption was it was probably something fairly minor but serious to him. Skylar had this way about him where he couldn't hide anything he had done that he thought was bad. He wasn't a tattle tell, except on himself. He would tell on himself. Skylar then proceeded to say he got in trouble at school. Knowing what I did about him I still assumed something minor had occurred. After all we hadn't gotten a call from his teacher. So I asked him what he got in trouble for. I tried to act stern as I always wanted our kids to know that getting in trouble at school was a serious matter. Skylar then answered me, "I said the F-WORD". I know my jaw dropped as I said, "You did what? He said it again, "I said the F-WORD". Mom began asking if he even knew what that meant. He replied in the affirmative and then added, "I called a girl the F-WORD". It then became a little bit of a blur after that as to what we felt and what we said. I know mom was exasperated and asked him again if he knew what that meant. I myself was afraid to ask. I mean what would he say or what sign language would he use to describe it? I thought I shouldn't have delayed in having THE TALK with him. I hoped he wouldn't answer. I was wrong. He was giving us an answer to mom's question. "Yes, I know what the F-WORD means, F-A-T, fat." Boy was I relieved. Now this wasn't okay, but it seemed less offensive in some respects. He was told he needed to apologize and he better not do this again. To this day the meaning of the F-Word remains the same to Sky and he knows not to use it. The rest of our family is probably more prone to use his F-WORD in describing someone. I'm not saying that's okay, it's not. I'm just making a point of once again how much we learned from Sky about caring for others and not offending them. I believe the whole world could take a lesson from him and others like him in that regard.

Too Far

I learned from one of my teenage granddaughters about the saying Too Far. She used it in a light hearted way when somebody would tease her a little too much or say something on the border line of being inappropriate. Most of our family can sometimes be brutal when teasing each other. It's not for everyone and we have to be careful with others around. For some reason we just lean toward sarcastic humor. That made us adopt the Too Far term; particularly when we could use it on the granddaughter that made us aware of it. I have to tell you of an incident that is a perfect illustration. You've probably figured out from some of the stories about Sky that he could possibly go, Too Far. It was hard to say it to him though as his borderline off color antics always seemed to most likely be unintentional. I say most likely because I wasn't always sure, particularly this time. It happened on a trip to Honduras. We were on a trip to do volunteer work at a girls' home and orphanage. The ministry was run by some friends of ours. When we first arrived we decided to go to dinner with them and some other people. Sky was in his early teens. As we were greeting people, some were meeting Sky for the first time. Sky went over to meet one particular young attractive lady. She wasn't real tall but Sky was fairly short for a teenager. It just so happened that the height ratios between her and Sky resulted in a potentially dangerous scenario; Sky's eyes met her chest high. Like I said, she was attractive. She also was well endowed and wearing a partially low cut blouse. Maybe this was like unintentionally throwing gas on a fire. As Sky greeted her his eyes widened and he got that familiar mischievous grin on his face. "What are those?" he said, "I like those"; so much for him "hating two". You know, he just called it like he saw it. Everybody laughed and as usual Sky got away with it. Shoot, in my younger days or any days for that matter, I'd never have gotten away with a comment like that. Whether Sky's comment was intentional or not, I must confess, he had gone Too Far, but also, I was impressed.

The Auction

Skylar sometimes had a subtle but intentional wit about him. If you hadn't been around him you would have thought certain occurrences were accidentally funny. I learned to know better. I'll give you an example. When Skylar was in high school we were invited to a fund raising banquet for one of the Associations he was a part of that helped Special Needs people. It was a typical banquet that would have dinner, speakers, some music, and then the sell and auction of donated items. We decided to sponsor a table and invited some family members to sit with us. The banquet was fairly good size and held in a large room at a Junior College. Skylar was selected as a greeter so he wore a suit. The program progressed accordingly and smoothly. As is pretty common at this type of event there was a kid running laps around the room during most of the speaking and auction. Normally this would never bother me. Because this time it was my granddaughter, it kind of did. I'm normally not embarrassed and had it been someone else's child or grandchild, I would have said it was cute and they are just being a kid. When I thought about the fact that she always called me Prince, I could still be a little embarrassed but not angry. I didn't even mind if she meant a Disney type Prince or the singer Prince. I liked him too. Nevertheless the auction continued. At some point I decided to bid on some items. I can be generous for a good cause but still tight with a buck, particularly when it's something you don't necessarily want. I did have a bid number and decided to bid on a few specific things. Like a careful gambler, I set a limit in my mind of the overall amount I would spend for the night. I bid on some items and wasn't successful. Being a tightwad, I was probably intentionally unsuccessful. I was then bidding on another item. It got to where just one other person and I were bidding against each other. I hadn't bought anything so I continued bidding by slightly raising the amount each time. I stopped after the item got over $300.00 deciding to let it go to the other bidder just like the earlier items that evening. Besides the live auction, there were also some silent auction items. Maybe I would donate by getting one of them. Then the auctioneer asked for the winning bidder's number. The response was a familiar voice; Skylar's. He said, Dad, what's our number? Then it dawned on me. Skylar had been sitting behind me at the same table and bidding against me. Not only that time but I learned he had also been bidding against me on some of the earlier items. He seemed pretty happy that he had beaten me and won the bid. When the evening was over and it was time to pay up I realized he had also won some of the silent auction items by placing last minute written bids. Maybe this kid is too smart. His tab was over $500.00. I jokingly said I should know better than to turn my back on him. I also thought this is the pitfall of having a higher functioning Down syndrome kid. Maybe the auctioneer should pay. He's the one that took his bid. Oh well, it was for a good cause. I was kind of proud of Sky that he could pull off such a feat right under, yet behind, my nose. I also asked my relatives at the table why they didn't stop him. Sky had that familiar smirk on his face that told me he knew exactly what he was doing and that he thought it funny. He'd hoodwinked me. Later I thought it's typical however. Not just of him and his comical nature but of all the kids like him. They would give it all. Not just money, but in care, laughter and love for others. How could you be upset with that? Another fun time, another lesson learned. Once again, a lesson learned by me.

Keep Laughing

Skylar's sense of humor always kept us laughing. I could tell a lot of stories of things he said and did but that might be sharing too much. Sometimes his humor was so matter of fact and even more evident of possibly bad parenting on my part; that it can only be shared with family and close friends. His mind for humor and laughing at almost anything was so close to mine that it could be embarrassing to tell more. Not embarrassing for him, but for me. For that reason I must end this chapter. So I will end it by summing it up that laughter is a big part of Skylar and his being. Laughter is good for not only the soul but also the spirit. Not just for Skylar's spirit. Not just our own either, but The Spirit of Mankind.

Hairy-Chested Man Contest Contestant; dance exhaustion.

Skylar “all blowed up” on steroids. Maybe eating 23 chicken nuggets and two pieces of lemon pie had something to do with it too.

Chapter 7

The Body

Body is defined as: the physical structure of a person. It can also be defined as: a group; together; collectively.

Preconception Can Be Misconception

Both definitions of body would become very important parts of Sky's life. Being born Down syndrome would definitely increase the chances that he would have certain physical traits but, as he would later preach, nothing is impossible with God. As Sky grew older he definitely started to change. The poor muscle tone that is typical of Down syndrome kids became less evident. He was shorter than most kids his age and wasn't as physically strong but his body was changing. We considered prayer as a big part of this. We also believe his involvement in Special Olympics made a big difference. When we first decided to get him involved we needed to search for a team. Probably my first thought about Special Olympics was how such a great organization could have been founded by someone that I imagined had totally opposite political views than conservatives like us. Now I didn't know anything about Eunice Kennedy Shriver, so I of course didn't really know her politics. I just had preconceived ideas. Unlike Sky and most people like him, I was like most every other, so called, normal person. I often prejudged people. As a Christian I of course shouldn't do this. I believe its cause is just sin nature born into man. But, one should work to overcome it. I believe God used Sky and many situations involving him to work on me. Though I still have very conservative views, I learned that it is more important to read people's hearts and intentions, above their perceived politics; once again, thank you Sky.

Facing Shortcomings

Soon the compassionate heart differences would be further reinforced through Special Olympics. I narrowed the team choice down and ultimately decided to try the team that was the largest in our area and had the most athletes. Not knowing how Special Olympics worked, I thought one negative of a large team might diminish his chances to perform. The positive of a large team was it could be a reflection of commitment by the leaders. When I saw the name of the main person in charge of the selected team, I noticed a familiarity. Being from a fairly large city, I thought surely this isn't the person I was thinking of. Now, the person in question had never done anything bad to me. It's just in sometimes dealing with this person over the years in business; I'd thought they were not the nicest. Surely this person that I thought was bossy, matter of fact, and not the most pleasant to deal with; wasn't the leader of this team. It's just someone with the same name I thought. Well, guess what? It was the same person. So, with trepidation based once again on preconceived ideas, we proceeded to become involved with the chosen team. Sky fit right in and had a great time, so did I. I also learned something else that resulted in a little shame on my part. This person that I had judged was not the person I thought, but one of the most compassionate, caring people I had ever met. Perhaps any negative thoughts I had in the past were my problem, not theirs. Once again, thank you Sky, for creating an opportunity for me to see my shortcomings and work on myself. Sky's involvement on this team with well over one hundred athletes would definitely help his physical development. The physical definition of a body was very positively affected. Through it, I was also affected. I once again had to face shortcomings. Face my own of course.

Remember Who It's For

The other definition of body, particularly this body of people, would have even greater effects. Sky started out participating in basketball. I don't remember a lot of unique moments but I do remember my first trip to the State Tournament. Traveling with a group of Special people numbering over 100 was a unique experience. It was a humbling pleasure. An even bigger impact on me is when we went to the Opening Ceremonies. As close to one thousand athletes marched into the stadium with their respective teams, I was emotionally impacted. There were also thousands of spectators and many coaches, family members, and friends. That weekend was an overflowing experience of every human emotion God gave to man. I believe I experienced every possible emotion that weekend. This experience ultimately combined to result in a joyous, memorable, life-changing experience.

You Are What You Think

Skylar later decided to try track. He liked it overall but, ironically, he really didn't like all of the running. He got used to that eventually. The other thing he didn't like was the cold. Track started in the spring and inevitably there would be a couple of cold weeks. One year he even quit due to the cold and all of the running. As Sky got older he began to like track more. The State Track Meet and Summer Games was a huge event. It was held at Wichita State University. Competitors came from all over the state to compete in many Olympics type events. I remember one particular race that Skylar was in. Athletes were pretty much paired in events by their qualifying times. Skylar wasn't a very fast or long-winded runner. He had gotten placed in a 100 yard dash event. Well, he could throw a softball and long jump pretty good but I knew this wouldn't be his event. Then I saw the line-up of other runners in his heat. They all looked fast. Two were over 6 foot tall. One teen was about 6'5" tall. Sky was only about 12 years old and less than 5 foot tall. I thought surely a mistake has been made. Skylar can't be in the same heat. Maybe he barely qualified for this bracket. It wasn't that I didn't have expectations; I did. I totally expected him to lose by a large margin; most likely 50 yards. I'd seen the television clips where a Special Olympian falls down and the others pick him up and walk together to the finish line. I didn't expect that to happen. It then became time to line up. The gun fired to start the race. Sky jumped right off the line and into an early lead. That didn't surprise me as Sky was smart and his small frame could be launched pretty quickly. To my surprise Sky started to build a sizable lead. I really expected the tall kid to be like a galloping giraffe and start to quickly close the gap with long strides. Well it didn't happen and Sky went on to win the gold. Sky wasn't a fast runner but from that time on he'd think he was. I figured that's okay because so much of who we are and what we accomplish in life comes through how we think and confidence in ourselves. Sky would go on to think he could do everything well and he had the confidence to do it. From telling the neighbor that he could ride a four wheeler, which he immediately wrecked, to weight lifting and many other things; Sky could do it. That confidence that was enhanced by Special Olympics would help him accomplish what was to me unimaginable. This included delivering a memorized short sermon at a National Fine Arts event and legally driving his car; things that to this day amaze me. What was a key ingredient in his accomplishments? Confidence was. I like to call it "God Confidence", where your confidence comes from the fact that God loves you the same as anyone else, and that with his help, you can achieve great things. It appears that confidence works for everyone, although you can possibly be over confident. I believe "God Confidence" is the best type you can have. I'm not sure, but I think Sky gets his directly from God. He may or may not exactly realize it and probably doesn't think about it, but I believe that somewhere in his spirit he understands the source. I hope that we can all encourage others to help build their confidence. Imagine what good might be accomplished for all mankind. .

Think Positive

For someone that faced a lot of obstacles, Skylar was really optimistic. Optimism however can't overcome everything that affects the body. I do think it helps. Sky had overcome being born with a heart defect thanks to modern medicine and prayer. His speech had gotten better by various physical therapies. Special Olympics had helped tone his body. Like many of us though, he was still plagued with a life-challenge that he had to deal with. I'm not talking about Down syndrome; I'm talking about Crohn's disease. At first we thought that he was just lactose intolerant when he started showing symptoms of quickly needing to run to the restroom. I thought it was pretty normal at first. After all, we have all been there. Also have you ever noticed the signs for restrooms in airports and a lot of other locations? They often look like a stick figure that is running. You don't have to be a genius to figure out why he's running. Now, I don't want to make light of Crohn's as it can be a very serious disease. Skylar continued to have problems, or "ploblems", as he called it. The doctor then thought it was most likely IBS (irritable bowel syndrome). As the "ploblems" became worse, it was decided to have him checked by a specialist. Without going into the details or discussing an exploratory procedure involving a hose in an undesirable location; Skylar was diagnosed with Crohn's disease. I could, in explaining the procedure, offer off color humor related to lines from Star Trek or Welcome Back Kotter; but, for now, I'll refrain. If you meet me and ask, I may tell. Making humorous or light-hearted remarks does not make conditions better but it can make them more bearable. It's a coping method that I have chosen to use many times in my life. I think it's one of the things Skylar used to deal with Crohn's. The other was prayer. Here was this young man that had faced so many things in his life; things that would have caused most people to give up. Yet, here he was being positive and optimistic. For some reason most people laugh at bathroom humor. It's really kind of sick and repulsive which may explain part of the complexity of the human mind and condition. Skylar realized that when he said he had "ploblems", he got a laugh. Without being graphic or disgusting, Skylar could deliver some funny lines relating to his condition. Many were intentional. Through it all he was positive. He never let Crohn's hold him back or keep him from doing anything. When younger he maybe didn't understand enough to be embarrassed in certain situations. As he got older he got better control of his symptoms and could avoid embarrassment. Through it all, his ability to think in the positive and be optimistic were astounding.

Call On The Best Physician

The other constant was prayer for his condition. Not only did he pray at home for healing but he raised his hand for prayer at almost every church service he attended. Even if it was suggested that he shouldn't always ask for prayer for himself but also pray for others; he would still ask for prayer. He prayed for other things too but he particularly prayed about his Crohn's. Skylar wanted healed and believed God could do it. If you asked him why he wanted healed it wasn't due to what you'd think. His answer was, he wanted caffeine. That may seem odd but due to his disease his caffeine intake was limited. This meant caffeine free soda, or pop as we call it. He was a self proclaimed "popoholic" and he wanted his pop in whatever form he wanted it. When a doctor told him he could have one pop per day containing caffeine, he had scored a victory. I don't know if I thought his disease was helped by prayer or not. Sky still had Crohn's disease, but it seemed to be better. Intravenous medications every 6 weeks had most likely helped. Consistent prayer had most likely helped too. Whatever the case or whatever you believe, Sky has gotten better. Maybe it's also mind over matter or laughter being a good medicine. Perhaps it is the combination of all of these things into a benevolent cocktail that worked for Skylar. No matter what happened, the point was, Sky believed he would get better and remained optimistic throughout his ordeal. To this day he continues to pray about his Crohn's. It's that simple child-like faith that amazes me. If we could all grasp just a portion of whatever it is that he has which helps him to deal with life, we would all be better off. He just lives his life to the fullest and is happy regardless of circumstances. Through observance of the many trials he has overcome in his physical body, I have realized what we can accomplish individually, but better yet corporately, through faith as one body; a Body of believers.

Skylar winning silver (to him gold), at Special Olympic

Chapter 8

The Heart

Heart is defined as: the innermost part of something.
As a verb: to like very much or love.

Be a Man

Heart may be a synonym for Skylar. Not only did he have his physical heart repaired, but the definition for heart fits him to a T; his love for others being the inner most part of him. He especially had a heart for girls. The self proclaimed "Ladies Man". That's Skylar all the way. I'm not sure when it happened but it was at a pretty young age. Now dad liked girls and his brothers liked girls, but Sky, really liked girls. He was and is totally girl crazy but in a different innocent way. I really can't put my finger on it exactly. He has this big incredible heart for people, just like most Down syndrome people do. Like he would say in his short sermon, "I love all people the same. God has given me this desire to love and to help others". So he loves everyone, but he likes girls. Maybe some stories will help explain his unique love of girls.

Unconditional Love

I cannot remember who it started with but the one who would span the longest period of time was Ainsley. From sometime in grade school to sometime in High School, this was his girlfriend. Oh, there were others here and there that also received the title, but she was a constant. What she ever did to be so highly honored, we may never know or be able to figure out. I did not know her very well but I could always sense a special spirit within her. Maybe this was what Sky picked up on with his special ability for loving people. Now it must be explained that being Sky's girlfriend did not always take a lot. Many were his girlfriend without ever knowing it. Often, if someone paid any attention to him, spoke to him, or even smiled at him, they would be named his girlfriend. But something was different with Ainsley. She was his girlfriend by being a girl and his friend; and yet to him their relationship was much more. I think we realized this when in grade school his teacher called mom about an incident at school. The teacher had noticed his girlfriend having something that looked a little out of place. For a girl to have an expensive piece of jewelry on, in early grade school years, would seem to be a little odd in most circles. A little questioning had revealed that Skylar had given the item to her and proposed marriage. Being a vigilant teacher, it was suspected that maybe the source of Skylar's material pledge should be investigated. It was an appropriate thought as the jewelry item did contain real diamonds and was of considerable value. It soon became apparent that Skylar had evidently become so enamored with Ainsley that he had procured one of Mother's jewelry pieces and hidden it in his pocket before school so he could pledge his love. I don't think that this was the first time I saw what I considered a deep vein of thinking in him. I did realize though that we needed to have a serious talk with him. This was in spite of the fact that I was also rather proud of him and the fact that he was smart enough to pull off such a caper. It also made me realize that maybe he was not the normal Down syndrome person and that his intelligence would require a more typical parenting vigilance of his actions as he grew. I would later think that maybe he was normal for Down syndrome; as I learned that though special, they are much more normal than most would think. Parental vigilance wasn't needed due to having a special child; it was simply a duty of being a parent.

Accept Others

Sky really was smooth with the ladies. Where he got it from I'm not totally sure. Although I would like to believe it was hereditary and in his DNA, I cannot rightfully take credit for it. I was never smooth like him. Some people are born leaders, others are disciplined, and many are passionate. Sky was smooth. I don't even know where he got all of his lines. Maybe we let him watch too much television. Maybe they weren't lines at all but just genuine comments. I remember pulling up to a convenience store with him when he was not yet a teenager. There were two teenage girls sweeping the walk in front of the store. They were the type he liked, cute. He definitely noticed them but I didn't know he noticed. As soon as we step out of the car near them, without missing a beat, he catches their attention. With a smile and twice raising the eyebrows, he simply says "hello ladies". They were smitten I believe. Possibly no young man had ever spoken to them with such sincere direct emotion. I could see their faces light up as if paid the greatest of compliments. We went into the store and after finishing our business left. Not another word was spoken to them; but I know, to Sky, they were his girlfriends. I believe in that brief moment due to his sincere flirtation, they also felt like they were his girlfriends.

Often when we were together, Skylar would spy a new girlfriend. Not one in the depth of his mind as Ainsley, but none the less a girlfriend for the current time; if only a moment in time. I wonder how many girls' self esteem Skylar may have affected in a positive way with his flirtations. Everyone knows that all ladies love a compliment; actually all people like a compliment. Sure there are different levels and needs in individual people for wanting acceptance. I believe everyone is searching for acceptance and a kind word can go a long way in helping to satisfy this basic human need. Like Sky's Trisomy 21, it's in our DNA. The need for acceptance is also in Sky's DNA and others like him. For Sky and many like him it seems much easier to show signs of acceptance to others. I know it's not my gift. Perhaps that ability is also in the DNA. If Sky's way of showing acceptance of girls is considered flirting, so be it. But maybe, just maybe, it's something much deeper and unselfishly innocent coming from him.

A True Ladies Man

I think all of his flirtatious moments however pale compared to one momentous occasion. The outcome of this event would reaffirm to me that God could put anyone in your path at any time. Additionally it would make me realize that if I ever wanted to accomplish anything big, Skylar would be my go to person. We aren't big concert or event attending people. We like people but crowds are not our favorite things. We are fairly set in our beliefs and would be considered very conservative by some. Mom unbeknownst to many has always been very politically minded. Through osmosis I became somewhat that way. It was however mostly mom that was the catalyst for going to this event. Mom had found out that Sarah Palin would be speaking at our fairly new city arena. This was a few years after her candidacy for Vice President of the United States. She was though, still a very popular and also polarizing figure. What amazed me about this event was that it wasn't for political purpose or for the city at large. It was open to the public but was actually a fundraiser for a local private Christian School. Skylar and his siblings had all attended Christian schools but not this particular one, although it was affiliated with the church denomination we attended. At first I thought it wouldn't be of much interest to me. Then I thought about the time that mom had wanted me to attend a speaking engagement of a politician who was The President. I had reluctantly taken her by car several hours away. I also voiced my opinion about not wanting to go and why. We weren't VIP's so we couldn't go on the political party's chartered bus nor have special seats. We had to stand several hours on the hard concrete. I later had to eat my words in a sense. After a strange chain of events we ended up standing about 20' away from George W. Bush during his speech. To top it off we shook his hand when he was finished as he walked by the crowd. I actually got a soul shake due to the position of my hand reaching over the person in front of me. I had to admit that was pretty cool. Thinking about that encounter made me consider that anything could happen at the Palin event. This time I thought we could hedge our bets on the possibility of meeting or shaking the hand of Sarah Palin. We are not star struck but I think it is human nature to be drawn to celebrity. As I'd said, the school hosting the event was part of a church of the same denomination we attended. Being that I had a lot of friends and knew many leaders in our denomination that attended there, I thought I might pull some strings. I actually thought it would be neat to meet the Palins but also neat for them to meet Skylar. Skylar was a high functioning teenager with Down syndrome and the Palins had a young son with Down syndrome. For some reason I thought it might be good for the Palins to meet Skylar. Maybe it could help them see some positive possibilities for their son. I remembered that when Skylar was little and we would meet a high functioning person with Down syndrome, it gave us hope for his future. One bonus was that if we did meet them, even though I was married to a very beautiful woman, I thought Sarah Palin would be "easy on the eyes". So, I set out to attempt arranging a meeting. I'm not good at asking for favors or taking charity but this time I was swallowing my pride and open to either. I was driven to try calling a few friends and leaders that I knew would be VIP's for the school at this event. Well, I struck out worse than a third grader facing a major league pitcher. I wasn't told no or sorry. My friends didn't even call me back. Oh well, I wasn't offended as I figured my asking was probably out of place anyway. The evening of the event came and we took our seats. Our sons didn't want to go but our daughter and daughter-in-law went with us. The event was at the new downtown arena. We had pretty good seats but they were on the side and up quite a few rows. We were at least 150 feet from the podium on stage. I could look down at the floor seats and see some of the VIP's; including friends I had tried to contact. On about the third row I noticed Todd Palin and their youngest daughter Piper. I am usually an over enthusiastic optimist so I decided to settle in and try to enjoy the evening, in spite of my failure to get a backstage pass. Sarah Palin came out and began her speech. It wasn't too long into the speech and an odd thing happened. I like to call it Divine Intervention or maybe it was just the beginning of a road to revenge. For some unknown reason, Piper Palin, "just happens to", look up into the crowd almost sideways over her left shoulder and notices Skylar. I don't think Sky knew who she was but it was just a girl who was maybe looking his way. He smiled and waved. For the next 30 minutes or more this innocent flirtation went on with both grinning and waving back and forth. Skylar, the notorious flirt, was putting his fingers to his ear giving her the call me sign. I'm not sure anyone else knew this was going on except those two and our family. Then at some point Todd and Piper were escorted backstage in what I assumed was in preparation for the closing of the event. I also assumed this was the end of the flirtation. I had however once again underestimated the power of The Sky Man. Piper Palin begins to peek out of the side curtains hiding the backstage area and continues the contact with Sky. She then steps out completely. At this time I assume some others in the crowd around us have noticed. It wasn't too long that someone comes down the stairs from behind us and says "she would like to meet him". My wife wanted to hear the rest of the speech so while the rest of us were taken back stage, they took mom down to an up close floor seat. For the next 20 minutes or so we sat back stage and talked to Piper, met Todd, and watched Skylar entertain Piper. She laughed a lot and I think she admitted it was probably the best time she'd had at one of her mom's speaking engagements. In a little bit my wife came backstage and said the speech was over and Sarah was thanking the crowd. I noticed a few of the VIP's huddled backstage most likely waiting to meet and take pictures with the Palins. A few people looked at us, I'm sure wondering what we were doing back there. To top things off, when Sarah Palin came backstage, she came and talked to Sky and our family before anyone else. We took pictures with their family before any of the other people backstage. Now I'm not one to gloat, but I thought it was pretty neat that we were the first ones to take pictures with them while the VIP's waited. I thought that's just how God often works as the great equalizer of people. Now all the people backstage were fine folks, many that I knew personally. I'm sure they didn't think of themselves as VIP's and didn't mind our being there. We sure weren't VIP's but I felt like God allowed Sky to be The VIP. Unexpected things could sure happen when my wife Paula invited me to an event. Considering what occurred unexpectedly at the separate Bush and Palin events, I thought that if Paula ever wants me to go see some celebrity speak again, I'll most likely jump at the chance to go. Furthermore, I realized that the next time I needed something done, I would be better off to not try and pull strings through friends or VIP's but trust the power of God and the special providence that he evidently bestowed on Sky. A year or two later we would meet Sarah Palin again at a book signing. Although Sarah wouldn't remember us, Piper did remember Sky. It was a brief meeting that confirmed Sky's power to make a lasting impression. I guess it also confirmed that he was right all along and really was: "The Ladies Man".

Another Special Love

Sky had other important girls in his life during High School. We heard often about Laura. Sky had met Laura at the lunch room. As he told it, she was sitting with some other girls and he went over and introduced himself. At some point he had talked her into taking a picture with him. That's how we first found out about her. It was by seeing her picture with him as the screen saver on his phone. Our daughter Alexis was working at the school and noticed that Sky would generally sit with Laura and some other girls at lunch. This didn't seem unusual as Sky was not bashful and after all, he did call her his girlfriend. From her picture on his phone, Laura looked to be a slim dark-haired beauty. This was not unusual as he did know how to pick them. We didn't know much about her. We did know she wasn't in Special Education classes. We also knew she wasn't really his girlfriend. We assumed she must be a nice person if she allowed him to frequently sit with her at lunch. That assumption would come to be a total underestimation of her character. One day our daughter overheard some conversation going on in the lunch room. Some girls were talking to Laura in a less than favorable manner about Sky's relationship with her and his calling her his girlfriend. Alexis, without her presence being noticed, heard Laura set the other girls straight. She told them that he was her boyfriend and that whenever he traveled he always brought her back a gift. We all know that he was a boy and her friend, but not really her boyfriend in common terms. But she made her point in standing up for Sky and not allowing their relationship to be made fun of. Now that far exceeds our assumption of her being a nice person. I'd say that is a person of compassion, integrity, and heart. It is not your typical teenager. For that matter it is not your typical person of any age. We finally met Laura once after a choir concert. Sky just had to introduce us. We made a point of thanking her for being so nice to him. I don't remember her exact answer but it was in the vein of, that she just liked him and wasn't doing anything special. Because of our inside information, we knew it was much more. She was special. Possibly we should have told her how we knew she was a special person but we never mentioned her conversation our daughter overheard. Laura and Skylar's lunch schedules would later change and not coincide so he saw a lot less of her. He was older than her and then graduated so he didn't get to see her, but he didn't forget. A year and a half after graduation he was still referring to her as his girlfriend and talked about marrying her; although I think she had a boyfriend. He usually made his comments with a grin and a raised pitch to his voice, so I think he knew that it wasn't a reality. I think it was his way of saying he wouldn't forget this person that was also special. Not as in Special Education, but in having a special heart for others. Cute probably paid a part in Sky selecting her, but I believe a bigger part was him having an innate ability to sense the true heart and spirit of others. He later told me that she was beautiful and he loved her from the moment he first saw her. I do believe Sky loved her just like he'd loved others before. He loved her, not like we often think of love. He loved her spirit with a pure love that has no lust or ulterior motive. I've heard of Agape Love but I like to think of this as Love to the 21st degree. A love somewhere based in that extra 21st chromosome.

A Special Gift

As graduation approached Skylar had another important relationship rekindled with a special person. The Special Education students could stay in high school until they were twenty one years of age or they could graduate after four years with kids their age. Many of the Special Education student's graduations were delayed by choice. Most liked school and seeing their friends. We later figured out that it was maybe a good thing for them to stay longer in high school. Nevertheless, the decision was made to have Skylar graduate after the regular four years. Typically the Special Education students walked together or by themselves at graduation. We were told that they could walk with other students if asked, but knew that rarely happened. We didn't mind Skylar walking at graduation with someone in his class, but there was not any particular close friend from his class graduating that year. It was just one more of those times in his upbringing where we didn't know what to do for him or how to help. We knew graduation was very important to him. We also knew that we would like him to walk with someone and not have to walk alone. It seems like it should be a simple thing to figure out. It wasn't simple and we just simply had no ideas. I'm not sure whether we prayed about it or not. Then something amazing happened, just as seemed to be normal in Skylar's life. I guess by now, having experienced so many amazing things happening in his life, I shouldn't have worried. I should have expected it. This time "it" was Elyse. She contacted Skylar's mother and asked if he could walk with her at graduation. Skylar had known Elyse since grade school. Like Skylar she was going to the same public high school. He saw her once in a while at school but really wasn't that close to her anymore. She had always been a sweet kid in grade school. Somehow she must have held on to that. Her act of kindness in asking Skylar to walk at graduation with her was impressive. Like many that have compassion toward others, I doubt that she thought of it as something special or a big deal. Let me tell you, IT WAS.

Love One Another

One more time in his life, Skylar could be normal like everyone else. We were so happy for him that he was able to fit in. I doubt that Sky gave it much thought as to how things worked out. I do think that if he would have had to walk alone, graduation would not have been the same for him. Someday he would have questioned why. As we watched his graduation I was moved by his inclusiveness due to Elyse's offer. At the same time my heart broke for some of the other Special Education students that were not afforded such an opportunity. Some walked alone and some walked with classmates. I believe that, like Sky, they probably didn't think anything about it. I did think about it. I have since thought that wouldn't it be a wonderful thing if someday the special needs kids were accepted as equal value by more of their classmates. Better yet, wouldn't the world be a better place if we all accepted each other as of equal value? The world has come a long way in regard to overcoming various forms of prejudice. Why can't we wipe it out all together and get to a place of equal value as proclaimed by the Bible? The Constitution of The United States simply proclaims that "all men are created equal"; though it has not always been practiced in its history. I believe the key to wiping out prejudice may lie within the special needs community. It is a community of people that, like Skylar, are accepting of all types of people. Also, other than when sensing evil, they tend to treat people equitably. I believe it is a God given trait that they have; to equitably love others. I believe it is a trait that needs to change in many of us. Not a physical change but a mental and spiritual change; a change, in our Heart.

Sky at Graduation with some of the family coming in behind him.

Sky being his usual entertaining self; backstage with Piper Palin.

The Palins were gracious to take a photo with our clan
"not VIPs"

Chapter 9

The Soul

Soul is defined as the spiritual part of a human being; regarded as immortal.
It is also defined as the essence or embodiment of a specified quality.

Just Dance

Of course, Soul is also often used to describe ones feelings or particular types of emotionally charged music. If you've read any of the first eight chapters of this book, I don't need to tell you, but I will. Skylar has a lot of Soul. It may be one of the best ways to describe him. Not only does it describe him in the spiritual sense but in the natural as well. He definitely has a deep spiritual side and spiritually soulful qualities. When it comes to music he is also full of soul. It seems to be an inherent trait with almost everyone I have ever encountered with Down syndrome. There is something special deep inside them that feels the music. I believe it is soul in their soul. Like the extra 21st chromosome that he possesses, it's a double portion of something in their physical, spiritual, and emotional makeup that makes them unique. Maybe it's this soul that made Sky love to dance. From a young age he would dance whenever he heard music. As he got older and attended functions with dances involved, he would try to be the first to hit the dance floor. I say try because often we would have to hold him back. Sometimes this was due to tradition, so the bride and groom could dance together first; other times so he wouldn't be the only one out there. He was not embarrassed or bashful. He danced with all of the brides, most of the bridesmaids, and strangers' girlfriends. There were many times when I saw him ask a lady to dance and off they would go. Meanwhile the lady's boyfriend or spouse sat alone at their table watching "their girl" walk away with Sky. I have wondered if they admired Skylar's ability and boldness to pursue the ladies. I sure did. Only someone like him or a really elderly man could get away with this. Since I don't have that extra something that Skylar has, I guess old age is my only hope. As Sky got older he knew all the line dances, took his solo turn in the middle of dance circles, and rarely left the dance floor. Sky really could dance for hours and he could dance well. Dancing was something he could do naturally as well as anyone. Sometimes he would even do a form of break dancing. Mom would tell him he could dance as long as he stayed off the floor. She didn't want Sky to be embarrassed. It didn't matter too much what you told him when it came to dancing though. Sometimes we would see him doing moves down on the floor but, if one watched closely, there were usually other guys of similar age that would at times be on the floor; particularly during specific songs. Sky had a big thing going for him too; he didn't get embarrassed. He did have the ability to be embarrassed by something on a rare occasion, but dancing was never the source. Some people don't like to dance; some may think it's a bad thing too. But, if you watched Skylar and others like him dance and saw the joy it brings them, there's no way you could think dancing was bad. The Bible says David danced before The Lord. I think God enjoyed David dancing, and David may not have even been a good dancer. I early on wondered why all of the Special Olympics big events had a dance? I soon learned why when I saw how much most of the participants loved dancing. It made them smile. It made me smile. If anyone ever looked like they were dancing for God it's these special people. I have no doubt that God has to smile when he sees Skylar and others like him dance.

Gifts from Heaven

A soul for music matters but the spiritual soul is of the utmost importance. The depth of Skylar's spiritual soul would be revealed over time. In the interim God would work on our souls. I can particularly speak to mine. God, it is said, works in mysterious ways. That's true. He also works in unique ways and at times when we least expect it. I was on a church mission's trip to Venezuela when the unexpected happened. It would bring me to tears and also comfort me in my concerns for raising Skylar. Our team of about 15 men was attending a church service in a church of several hundred people. It was a service that we weren't even supposed to be at. Our team of men had gone to Venezuela on a construction mission's project. A couple of days prior to our scheduled return home a Hurricane in the Atlantic Ocean was headed possibly toward southern Florida. Our scheduled return flights were routed through Miami. Well, this resulted in many flights being canceled and rescheduled. It would cause our teams return to be broken up with our rescheduled return flights being one to three days later. It was this delay that resulted in our being at this church service. Before the service I noticed a boy with Down syndrome. He was, I guessed, about 10 or 12 years old. He was walking and running around the room. Even after the service started he was still up front walking around. He wasn't unruly but seemed out of place. He appeared to be a little restless and I wondered if they would just let him run around the whole service. It was a little distracting and a little comical. Then, after about five minutes, it happened.

Of all the people in the church, this young man looks directly at me, smiles, and heads toward me. He then proceeds to sit on my lap and put his arms around my neck. The tears began to stream down my cheeks as he sat there. I hugged him back as I thought about Sky. More importantly, I thought about God's reassurance to me. It is not coincidence when out of several hundred people; a young man with Down syndrome picks out and shows love toward a man who is wondering how to best raise his own young son with Down syndrome. It's kind of like the Piper Palin meeting. Maybe Sky came to the Palin family at a time when something was needed, just as this young man came to me. I don't remember anything else from the young man in Venezuela except that I was the only one he picked out. After a few minutes someone came and got him to take him to his seat. I was hoping the family wouldn't be embarrassed by what he had done. I more so hoped they would be told what God had used their son to do for me. This reminded me that God has often used sons to send messages; His son, my son Skylar, and now this Venezuelan son. It always seems to be at unexpected times and exactly when someone needs it. Some people may think this is coincidence or chance. I like to think of it as little gifts; gifts from Heaven.

Pray

Skylar knows how to pray. In fact I think he has an unexplainable, simple, and direct line to God. After all, prayer is just talking to God. It doesn't have to be long or elaborate. In fact sometimes more seems to be accomplished with the simplest of prayers. Maybe God is so busy with desperate prayers for help and the sheer volume of prayers that he appreciates it short, simple, and to the point. It sure seems like he has answered a lot of my prayers at the last minute or when I thought I was at the end of my rope, so to speak. Maybe, if folk's prayers were shorter and to the point, He'd be able to get to mine in a timelier manner; I'm just kidding God. Well, like I said, Sky knows how to pray. Sky also likes to be prayed for. Almost every time that he's at a church and it's asked who needs prayer, he raises his hand. Oh he will pray for others too, but he loves to be prayed for. When he was little I thought he did it for the attention. He always had a special connection with our Pastor. If there was prayer at the altar at the end of a service, Sky would always be down front. I would then see him move around to strategically place himself where the Pastor would see him; hoping to get prayed for. He'd do a lot of peeking and sometimes move several times. You're probably not supposed to peek during prayer but who am I to pass judgment. I was peeking too. At some point, Pastor would see him and pray for him. Once he did, Sky was content and his prayer time was over. Sky however also returned the favor, particularly as he got a little older. In fact he was the only kid and one of the few people, period, that would boldly go to the altar and pray for the Pastor. I think Pastors as the spiritual leaders in a church are often respected and looked up to. It can be a little intimidating to the rest of us to go pray for them. Maybe it's because we think; how could my lowly prayers help them? They are at a much higher spiritual level. Now I knew in my mind that they are just people like the rest of us. I did have a respect for them, particularly our Pastor. I mean, I felt a little intimidated about praying for him. I did pray for him, but most often in a group when prayer was requested for him. It didn't make sense that it was difficult to boldly go pray with the one mentor that had taught me the most about prayer. Maybe that is one of the reasons that Skylar was brought into my life by God; to help teach me to be bolder about praying for our leaders and that they are just equals with us in the eyes of God. In my having a love for history I had heard it said about a gun brand in the Old West that "Colt was the great equalizer". In relation to men fighting, it was. It didn't matter whether you were the biggest or strongest physically in a fight. If you both carried a Colt you could, in a sense, be equals. Well, really, God is the great equalizer. I believe, He made us all and we are equals in birth, death and the choice at eternal life.

Sky's boldness to pray with the Pastor and how he treated others reinforced this fact. Sky really did treat people as equals. It seemed a little ironic when I thought about this and that many years earlier Skylar's older brother was named Colt; yet Sky would be the great equalizer. An equalizing force in reforming the way we looked at others.

Black Hurleys

Something else affected Skylar somewhere deep in his soul. He was intrigued by funerals and death. It wasn't quite like you'd expect though. From an early age he had a fascination for funerals. He would watch the funerals of famous people on TV and want us to tape them (remember tapes?). He would then watch them over and over. He watched funerals for Ronald Reagan, Pope John Paul II (The Pope-ee as he called him), Michael Jackson and many others. He somehow also watched reruns of funerals for Mother Teresa and Princess Diana. He once was trying to tell me about one of the funerals and he kept asking me about the "Black Hurley". I finally, a couple of funerals later, figured it out when he said, "You know, the body. Why do they always put it in the Black Hurley?" I realized he meant the hearse. Now you may be wondering what kind of parent lets their kid watch televised funerals. Well it gets worse, or better, depending on how you look at it.

The Box

I guess I assumed that Sky had a child like mind and wouldn't be affected by death or think about it deeply. That is probably why I didn't mind. It's also probably a part of the reason why we began letting him go to funerals of people we knew. Of course he asked to go many times before we let him go; particularly as he got a little older. One of the first funerals he went to was for an older lady in our church. I was curious as to how Sky would react and what questions he may ask. I told him that the body was just the container and that she was no longer in there. I told him that I believed she was in Heaven. Things were pretty uneventful and Sky didn't have any tough questions. At a later date he did. I don't remember if it was a few days or a few weeks. I believe it was at bedtime when we'd generally tuck him in and say prayers. He asked me, "Why did they put Granny in a box?" It wasn't his real Granny but the preferred name of the lady who had passed away. It seemed like an odd question but a very serious question to Sky. I explained again about Granny really not being in there and it was just her body while on Earth. I really didn't have a good answer. All I could say is that the casket, "box", was the container used to bury the body. I guess I'd never wondered why funerals and burials were done that way. Sky's question really had a lot of wisdom in it. Why is it done that way? Secondly, if we believe it's just a body and not the person's soul, isn't it just a box?

Peace Out

I remember another funeral in particular at our church. The funeral was for an older man in our church. It wasn't someone Sky really knew. At the close of the funeral they had a viewing line pass by the coffin. True to form, Sky slipped away. I noticed him in the line, although I think we'd told him to stay seated with us. Not wanting to cause a disruption, I just watched Sky from a distance. He paused by the casket and leaned in a little. I later asked him what he was doing down by the casket. He said, "I just wanted to talk to the guy". Sky then, while bouncing off his chest a peace sign formed with his fingers said, "I told the guy, peace out". Further questioning revealed that he had given him the hand sign too. It struck me as funny at the time. Sky was just being Sky but not really understanding. However, as time went on and I thought about it more; I thought maybe Sky had it right. To a Christian man that believed in his

Heavenly Destiny, Sky had pretty much summed it up. A simple truth had been declared in two simple words. I came to believe that no better sentiment could have been achieved in a long eulogy by a Preacher, Diplomat, Author, Poet, or other gifted public speaker.

Am I Next?

Sky took his funeral fascination a little further when he started using me as the dearly departed. Sometimes it happened at his bedtime when I'd lay beside him to say prayers. It sometimes happened if he saw me lying on the couch or leaned back in a recliner. He'd cross my hands over my chest; do the crosses sign over my head, shoulders and chest; kiss both cheeks, and then lay on top of me and fake crying. He'd moan loudly and say, my father is dead, he's passed away. Finally he would break out into singing Amazing Grace. It was pretty entertaining. If the antics and crying weren't bad enough, the singing was. Sky has a lot of gifts, but singing isn't one of them. Sky would always have a smirk on his face during his performance, even when fake crying. It's another one of those mysteries as to where he comes up with this type of thing. He probably got some of it from watching the Pope. Sky would often do the cross and a similar cheek kiss to me and say he was the Pope. The crying and singing he probably got from the various funerals he had watched. His presiding over my, thankfully pretend, funeral was eventually done to me so much that it wasn't as entertaining. It began to seem a little creepy. As I got older, I quit being such a willing corpse and this phase mostly passed. Mostly I say, because years later he occasionally pulls it from his bag of tricks and I become the dearly departed once again.

Is This All?

I don't think Sky really thought about me dying some day. Neither do I think he really understood or contemplated the death of himself or others. Of course none of us understand death but we do contemplate it. Sky's using me as his corpse, though funny, did make me consider my own mortality. It made me to more deeply consider how my death could affect his life. I felt more compelled to think about ways to secure his future once I and his mother were gone. All of these stories that I have related helped to make it clear that Sky had a fascination with death. I searched my own soul for answers to explain death to him as best I could someday. I pretty much came to the conclusion that I wouldn't have to try. I felt relieved. Although I knew he seemed more intelligent than many kids with Down syndrome, I had concluded that surely his thinking

process was not complex enough for him to be deeply thinking about death. It seemed his thoughts about death were more like a game at times or a series of comical and weird movie scenes. Once again, I underestimated Skylar. He was about 19 years old when I realized how much. As we lay in his bed about to say prayers he suddenly said, "Dad, I don't want to die". Wow, I thought, where did that come from? This was followed by real tears streaming down his face. I believe he was intensely feeling that fear of the unknown that all of us face. Christian or not, if we are honest with each other, the thought of our own death is sometimes troubling. I choose to believe in an afterlife and that when I die that's not the end of me. I don't understand where I was before I was born. Who can understand not existing? I don't totally understand where I'm going either. But there have been too many things that have happened in my life that have affected me in a positive way; that reinforce my faith. They can't be just chance. Skylar's existence has been one of the most influential. I refuse to believe his life was an accident or chance. It is moments like Sky's facing death and all of these mentioned that moved my soul. My soul was refreshed and my faith strengthened. These moments and many others led me to believe; Sky's extra 21st chromosome gave him
something extra, something extra in his Soul.

Skylar being prayed for by Pastor Jon Hollis

Chapter 10

The Future

The Future is defined in some dictionaries as: that is to be; specifically: existing after death.

Perfect Timing

No one on earth knows their future. Though we think and maybe dream about our futures, we are not assured of the next breath or heart beat. All men, and sorry ladies but this includes you, are destined to die. We also tend to plan for our futures. There is nothing wrong with that but other than eternal life through Jesus Christ, which I believe in, I know of no other way of being assured of anything in one's future. Even this book's future was not assured. The plan was to write it sooner and about the early years of Skylar's life followed by a sequel about High School and beyond. This chapter was to deal with discussing what might occur in his future, including High School and the possibility of College. Well, time often gets by us. High School has happened and Skylar is actually attending College. Maybe I was just being lazy in not writing about his life sooner. Oh, believe me, there has been plenty of interesting material. I'd like to think that my procrastination was guided by God to align with his timing. Like anyone, I sometimes put things off although I'm not really geared to do so. I have often wondered why I was being slow in accomplishing a certain task. The longer that I have lived I have noticed that when I have delayed a project unintentionally, I can always look back when it is complete and see the essence of perfect timing. I have learned to be patient in most circumstances and trust in God for his perfect timing. It always works best and makes life easier.

Deliver a Message

I know that Skylar has a bright future. I feel it deep inside of me. From the time he was a little boy, I always felt he would someday speak to people and tell his story. Little did I know that he would develop a gift of gab and a memory to be able to deliver a speech. He was not very verbal as a small child. I'm not sure I ever thought of it until now, but somewhere along his life path, he totally changed. It is almost impossible to keep him from talking to people. Everywhere he goes he wants them to know his life story. Likewise, he wants to know about them and their life. He is genuine and sincere. This is a prized public speaking skill. I saw it in him during his short sermon at a National Fine Arts event that I mentioned in an earlier chapter. The theme for the Fine Arts was "Limitless". He had delivered his speech well enough in our home state that he was advanced to the National Event. There were over 10,000 people in attendance at the convention with competitors in multiple events. There were several hundred in his event alone. Sky basically told about his life. His major scripture was Jeremiah 29:11 NIV, For, I know the plans I have for you, declares The Lord, plans to prosper you and not to harm you, plans to give you hope and a future. Skylar's older sister wrote the sermon for him and refined it to fit his speaking abilities. The maximum time limit was 5 minutes. Skylar's was about 4 minutes long after he practiced it over and over. Early in the process I had started to doubt that he would be able to pull it off. He really struggled with the words and memorization. At some point, as was his typical pattern, it sunk in and he had it. I felt a little ashamed that I doubted him. Normally, I optimistically supported him and thought he could do anything. But, for some reason, this wasn't one of those times. The day then came for him to deliver his sermon at the National Fine Arts event. There were about one hundred people in the room. We entered the room about two speakers before Sky. Prior to his turn and true to his norm, Skylar goes up front and talks to the judges. I later found out that he had asked one of the judges if he would give him a good score. With most we would call this an attempt to "grease the judges". With Sky, talking to the judges is just an honest, sincere gesture of kindness. There is no alternative motive. Then it was Sky's turn. The crowd consisted of about 20% family and friends, with the rest being strangers. In the many years that our older kids competed in Fine Arts, we only saw one kid compete that had Down syndrome. He was in the competition for a couple of years in an event called Human Videos. I believe Skylar was probably the first in this particular category. We knew he could pull this off but I'm sure most in the room were curious about what was to come. We were also curious because with Sky you really don't always know what's going to happen. When Sky started, he said his name. Then he said, "Before I start, I just want to say something". He then makes a short statement about having been born in his mom's tummy. This was a total ad lib and seemed entirely out of place. I'm sure the judges and the crowd now thought they were about to here a total bust. The wife and I were also a little concerned. Then he gets on track and starts his speech. We should have never doubted Sky. He delivered that sermon the best he ever had. It was clear, to the point, and emotional. He drove it home with particular dramatic emphasis when he delivered the final sentence; "I'm sure I had doubters, but God never doubted me, for he has made me LIMITLESS". Sky got a standing ovation that day and at least half the audience had tears in their eyes; even a friend of ours that was normally reserved and stoic, had tears in his eyes. Sky didn't finish in the top ten but he did get rated in the highest category resulting in finishing in the top third. I had hoped that he would be selected to deliver his speech at the closing ceremonies for over 10,000 people. I think it would have been powerful, but it wasn't meant to be. This did inspire me to think that he may speak to big crowds, in the future. It just wasn't His time yet.

Driving

Driving was another thing that I dreamed for Sky's future. I would never have thought of that ever being possible had we not run into a family years earlier that Paula slightly knew. Sky was probably less than 5 years old. This family had a 20 year old daughter with Down syndrome. As we talked they told us she drove with a restricted license. Like most people, I'd never heard of such a thing. Because of this "chance" meeting, I began thinking of the possibility of Sky driving some day. I didn't count on it but it gave me hope. Sky loved cars. From a young age he loved Corvettes, particularly red convertible Corvettes. I'm not sure how, but Sky always recognized Corvettes of almost any model year. He was only about six or seven years old when he started pointing them out. He couldn't even read but somehow he knew. I thought maybe it was the racing flag emblem. When he was about 10 years old, he called a local dealer to inquire about a particular corvette he'd seen in a newspaper ad; next to the dealer's phone number. I don't know what they told him but Special or not, that's an enterprising kid. As Sky got older he became particularly adept at video games, particularly driving games. All of these prior events helped reinforce in me that possibly some day he could drive. As he got closer to driving age I'd sometimes let him drive an old pickup on our property. He was short so I'd sit in the middle like a postman and operate the gas while keeping one hand on the wheel. When he was about 15 years old, mom would let him drive her car sometimes on a back road by our house and even let him pull it in the garage. When he was 16 I purchased a rather expensive sports car. I promised him that he could be our first child to drive it. When we picked it up from the dealer we proceeded across the street to an empty parking lot to fulfill the promise. I sat in the passenger seat and took a video of him as he made multiple oval circuits around that lot. It was much to the chagrin of one of our older sons that I let Sky drive that car, but I did have him maintain a very slow pace. Sky drove on our property and a little on the back road for a couple of years. When he was 18 years old I thought he was ready to drive more and hoped there was a way for him to get a learner's permit. Eventually I was referred to an instructor at a driving school that would work with him. If you enrolled in the class you would get a legal learner's permit. Sky spent several months going once a week for an hour lesson. His instructor that owned the school was a wonderful man. Although Skylar probably drove as good as our other kids had when teenagers, it scared me nearly to death. It had been a long time since I had ridden with a teenager learning to drive. I learned to sit in the back and mostly look down at whatever electronic or reading diversion I had brought; while we sped down the road. Sky's instructor was the most laid back, trusting, and relaxed individual I think I had ever met. He mostly talked in a calm voice to Skylar while he occasionally eased him back on the right path. Not only did he teach Sky a lot about safe driving, he taught me that being a driving instructor was a definite skill; a skill that I did not possess. Skylar progressed so much that I felt comfortable enough to consider getting him a car that we could practice in. I discussed a car purchase with mom. I think she preferred "an old tank" that would be really safe in a crash. I assumed she meant maybe a 1970's Ford LTD, or being a typical overprotective mother, maybe she thought an actual army tank. I envisioned her thinking about a car with tires strapped around it like W.C. Fields in The Road Hog. Whatever the case, I had a bright idea. Why not get him a car and make it safer by adding one of those brakes on the passenger side, like the Drivers Education cars. Better yet, why not get him some kind of neat car and add the brake. Even better yet, why not get him the kind of car he's loved since he was little and put one of those brakes in it. I started looking for him a car. I didn't really think it would happen. I looked for older cars to keep the price down but I wanted something in decent shape. Some of the family knew of my secret mission and helped look for a car. I was afraid of mom talking me out of the purchase, thinking it to be too dangerous, so I opted not to tell her. I do not recommend doing this. We were blessed to find a nice 24 year old car in great shape for a great price. I still questioned the purchase but then thought why not. I thought, he has wanted a car for a long time and the price is less than we'd spent on getting cars for our older kids; this being true with the exception of, and reminded by, our oldest son (you know how it is, you're poor with the older kids). Because it was for Sky, I believed he would forgive me. Mom could be another matter, I thought. For Sky to drive his own car would be a major milestone in his life. A milestone that I had at one time never imagined would actually happen. Presenting the car needed to be a big deal, so a plan was made. I had finally told mom about the purchase. All of the family was invited for his birthday and the big reveal. Our business had a big yellow box truck that I had given a particular name. We parked that truck in a manner so as to hide the car. We brought Sky outside with the rest of the family. Then mimicking a certain television shows big reveal, in a somewhat strange way, I announced, "Move that big yellow turd". Our son-in-law pulled the truck forward and there sat the car with a big red bow on it. It was his long loved favorite; a shiny red Corvette convertible. He was elated; maybe I even more. Tears of joy welled up in my eyes as I celebrated this accomplishment with him. The passenger brake got installed and as of this writing, we have not crashed the car. Sky doesn't want to drive a lot but we've probably traveled over 1,500 miles with him behind the wheel. One day we took an excursion out of town and traveled well over 100 miles round trip. This too has inspired me for his future and the future of others. Maybe Sky being able to drive will be an inspiration for the future accomplishments of others like him.

So Much for Driving

No, he didn't crash. Yes, the driving mostly stopped; temporarily I believe. Sky drove for about two and a half years, until I made a mistake. In hind sight maybe it wasn't a mistake and I was protected from a potential legal nightmare. In further thought it may have been best for Sky. I didn't think Skylar was ready for a full license. I really envisioned a lifetime learner's permit. Some way I heard that a learner's permit was maybe only good for one year. The one Skylar had from the driving school didn't say. It was a paper form and was getting a little tattered. I decided to take Skylar into the DMV to get a new permit; the normal card type with a picture. They said getting one would be no problem. They also immediately confiscated the paper one he had and informed us it was only good for a year. There might even have been some talk about some illegal driving for the last year and a half. It wasn't us! I mean all of us criminals say we didn't do it. We then went through the process of filling out documents, providing an eye test, and having his picture taken. Then the lady says he has to take the test now. I said, "What test"? I was told, the written test. When I got a learner's permit you didn't have to take a test. You only took a written test when getting your driver's license. I found out that the process was now reversed and the written test had to be passed before getting a learner's permit. Now I knew my granddaughter, who was a gifted student, had taken that test recently. She studied a lot and had to take it twice to pass. I also thought, I know of a lot of people that are driving that have a lot less comprehension of the English language and are a lot worse drivers than Sky. In fact, I passed some of them every day on the road. They tried to be helpful and said they could give him the test orally. I said he won't pass and he's not ready to take a test. We got the driving handbook for him to study and I inquired about an audio handbook. Of course there isn't one. Not sure of how Sky could pass the test and more concerned with him just being able to legally practice driving; I decided to contact the driving school he had attended to see about getting another learner's permit through them. The owner of the school said that the State had really cracked down on his business and made it virtually impossible for him to issue a permit. The driving school's inability to issue a second permit leads to another roadblock in our lives. This was another where we didn't know what to do. I mean, it's really frustrating to drive for two and a half years and then not be able to; particularly if you've not done anything wrong (other than unknowingly driving on an expired permit). My thoughts of an easy solution became non-existent. The positive thing was it made me consider that possibly Skylar could take the test and pass. I even thought I should have just let him take the test while at the DMV. Maybe he would have passed by Divine intervention. I decided to give him the handbook and some practice tests. We also found him a tutor to work with him a couple days per week for a few months. Sky surprised me as usual. I realized he was spending a lot of his time in our basement foregoing video games to study the book. By a combination of his being tutored and reading the questions himself, he was virtually memorizing the practice tests questions and answers word for word. I really don't know how.

Maybe that was Divine intervention. In spite of all that occurring, I still wasn't sure how exactly to proceed. Once again someone was put in our path as a person that may help. An initial phone call resulted in Skylar being accepted back into a High School summer driver's education program. He will be with regular education students and the instructors will help him. He will have to pass the written test and each portion of the driving test. If so he will obtain a standard driver's license. From what I've witnessed so far, I now believe he can do it. As of this writing he's a couple of months away from possibly doing the unexpected and getting a driver's license. I may have doubted him but like his short sermon said, God never doubted him. Better yet, Sky doesn't doubt himself or his ability through Him.

Higher Education

What can I do for the future needs of my Special family member? I asked myself this question many times as I'm sure other families do. We all ask the same question about our so-called "normal" children too. Often we dream of higher education. Although my wife and I had limited higher education experiences, it was still something we desired for our children. On the one hand, my father had done pretty well having come from the farm and only completing 8th grade. I thought I had done pretty well having survived and completed only one boring semester of college. For our kids though, we wanted more. The high school that Skylar attended was attached to a branch of a local community college. I began to envision Skylar possibly being able to take a class or two there once he graduated. Maybe he could handle a basic art class or something that didn't necessarily have to involve a lot of study. I thought something simple would be possible. While in high school Skylar began to ask about going to college. He often said he wanted to go to college in Texas like his older brother had done. Of course that becomes a difficult question to answer. You can only divert answering so many times by changing the subject or giving a vague answer like "maybe". His continued questioning caused me quite a bit of internal anguish. We opted for Skylar to graduate at the normal time rather than stay in high school until 21 years of age as many Special Education students are allowed to do. I thought I would go over to the community college to discuss him attending but like many good intentions in life, it didn't happen. The fall semester was upon us and Skylar really didn't have a lot of daily activities planned. Now, he was just fine playing video games all day but as fairly decent parents we didn't want that to be his routine. I was feeling guilty that I had procrastinated and not pursued something for him. I tried to comfort myself by thinking I could get him in next semester or next year. I also selfishly thought that if he wasn't tied down we could travel more together for work and pleasure. This of course did nothing for his desire to attend college. Then, out of the blue, another one of the amazing things that just seemed to appear from nowhere in Sky's life, happened. I was contacted by a lady that said she remembered our saying something about Skylar wanting to attend college. She told me that a new program was being started by a lady and gave me the contact information. I immediately contacted the lady that had started the program although I knew regular college classes had already started. I assumed it was some kind of short class at the community college. Then something happened, more so as had become usual when dealing with things in Skylar's life, something extra happened. Not only were their two spots left, but he could enroll even though the class had started. Furthermore, not only would he be going 6 hours once a week, similar to other students, but the program was at an accredited University. The program would include an adult curriculum for Special Education students and a lot of interaction with other university students. The class intent was to give Special Education students the opportunity to have a college experience and to further introduce and encourage interaction between regular and Special Education students. At this writing Skylar is in the second year of the Friendship Fields program at Friends University.

We, as parents, feel indebted to the lady that was responsible for creating this program. Her tireless work and compassion for what some consider the less fortunate is to be commended. Hopefully others will learn of this program and emulate it so others like Sky can have a college experience. While this program filled a void in Skylar's desire to attend college it also brought more questions from him in regard to his future. Now he says he has to go to college for four years and then will graduate. That is currently not part of the program and seems impossible, but as I've learned in helping navigate Skylar through life, the impossible often comes to pass in an extraordinary way. If this hope for the future comes to pass, I'm sure it will further inspire others to believe in the impossible being possible, for their future.

Pursuing Dreams

Future provision for any family member is on almost every parents mind. Just like the mighty eagles that feed and care for their young and later help them learn to hunt for food and survive on their own; we have an innate desire to provide for and later train our offspring to provide for themselves. Future provision for the meek, elderly, and handicapped tend to be more difficult. No one wants to leave a situation where someone is a burden on the rest of the family or left to depend on society at large for subsistence. Nevertheless, it happens. Both my wife and I did not want this to happen with Skylar. I knew that Skylar could work in our construction company in some capacity. I thought this would be better than some menial task through a job program. Now I'm not against job programs; sweeping, taking out trash, making brooms, or any other task that may seem of lower importance. All jobs are important no matter what level of importance or value is placed on them by some people. They should be considered valuable and done to one's best ability. But like most parents, I wanted more for my son. I thought that we had the wherewithal and resources to create something that would allow Skylar to contribute in a meaningful way toward his future provision. If successful he could be taken care of, not be a burden on his siblings, and possibly be an inspiration to others, long after I was gone. I'm not sure you can go to your grave happy or with a smile on your face but I could maybe get close. This is when the idea for Sky's was born. Why not start a business that could be named after Sky with some of the profits being used to support his future life needs. Better yet, maybe we could use a portion of the profits to help other Special Needs people and programs. We also envisioned providing some work opportunities to some Special people and help further the general publics' understanding and compassion for people like Sky. The idea started as a breakfast and lunch restaurant with a pretty modest budget. It would be operated by Sky's sister and brother-in-law. Maybe we could start in a rented space or convert an old house. Through a series of delays and setbacks the vision evolved into buying a building, then later to building our own building and expanding the business to an event venue also. It became a project that would in essence "bet the farm". I would show Sky the picture of Colonel Sanders on the Kentucky Fried Chicken signs and tell him, if successful, he would be like that guy. He would be the good will ambassador and national spokesperson. Why not try this. After all, Sky would be a great spokesperson and advocate for Special People. He talks to everyone and would be a great promoter. I believed that if it was meant to be, we worked hard at the dream, did it for the right reasons, and were patient to wait on God's timing; it would succeed. As I write this we are still in the process of making this dream become a reality. Possibly, as you read this we have begun building or operating. In the interim, through what I consider a miracle, Skylar was hired at a Chick-fil-A restaurant. After spending a lot of time in our basement playing video games, I wasn't sure how he would do. He'd work in our office some but generally after about an hour he would clock out and say he'd worked a long time. I've been told by several people that he does a great job at Chick-fil-A and works hard. He's gone to work as early as 7:00 AM and worked as many as 7 straight hours. He mostly delivers food to tables and of course talks to everyone. I believe it is great training for his future dream of owning a restaurant. I am proud of the job he is doing and I know that he would be the best at customer service in his own business; simply because he loves everyone.

Whatever the case and whatever God has in store for us, we will openly accept it. We will accept it and never stop dreaming about the future and never stop encouraging others about their future.

Don't Spend Life Alone

Sometimes being alone is not a choice. Although everyone at times says they want to be left alone, I believe man is best when not left alone. I think that man has an innate nature to have fellowship with others. Skylar and his peers are no different in this regard. I have witnessed many people that sacrificially give of their time and talents to help Skylar and others to fit in and be accepted. Many years ago a person with Down syndrome would most likely have been put in an institution for the mentally handicapped. As time went on, this began to change as more people became advocates for their acceptance in society. In our country a book by celebrities (Roy Rogers and Dale

Evans), Special Olympics, an increase in awareness, medical progress, and acts of Congress (Americans with Disabilities Act) were just a few of the things that played a part. Yet with all of those progresses and programs, there are still hurdles to be overcome. Special needs people are still often segregated. Skylar could generally fit in well with people. Sometimes his thinking was a little different and he may do something that someone may think irritating. Typically though, I came to realize it was a cry for attention and to be accepted. From observation over many years, I realized this was true of many people with Special Needs. In fact it is true of everyone; it is just expressed differently based on a variety of factors. One place that Skylar was misunderstood was church. We went to a very loving church for many years prior to Skylar's birth. When he was born and through his heart surgery, the leaders and people were there for us. We could never express enough gratitude for how we were cared for and prayed for. As he got older and differences between him and others his age became more apparent, Skylar was less accepted by some. When he became a teenager and as is typical, he wanted to sit with the other kids and not with us. This almost always resulted in him sitting across the aisle from us; alone. It broke my heart. Now, I didn't fault the church or other kids. It just was what it was. He was different and people tend to gravitate toward those they have the most in common with. Also, teenagers are teenagers. I may have done the same thing as a teen. I often hoped and prayed that someone would sit by him or invite him to sit with them. Other than a youth pastor, it was rare. If it did happen, typically it was a newer kid in church or someone lacking popularity. I never said anything and it really didn't bother Skylar. It broke my heart yet I understood and used the experience as a study of mankind. The more I watched Skylar and others with Special Needs interact with people in school and other situations, I noticed a sense of loneliness. I came to believe that the greatest prejudice that we have yet to overcome is that toward the mentally and physically handicapped. I also came to realize that there are lots of lonely people that spend time alone mostly due to being different.

My goal is to make a difference in that regard. I'm not the most social person and like some time alone, but I do like acceptance by others. I may sometimes choose to be alone as I believe Skylar does also. My prayer is that Skylar won't be alone in the future; particularly when he wants and needs the acceptance and fellowship of others. I pray this for others like him too. In fact I pray this for everyone; the physically impaired, the elderly, the poor, those some consider undesirable, and even those who appear to have it all together. Often, they are lonely too.

Someday, I hope for Skylar to have a wife. A wife both

for companionship and so he'll never be alone. He loves girls and wants a girlfriend, maybe more than one; but I know he also wants to someday have a wife. He talks about it quite a bit. Not quite as much though as he talks about moving out. I don't want him to ever go. If it's his desire to, we will trust God for a way to fulfill that for him. Hopefully Skylar won't move out until he is married. I'm sure Skylar will be a good husband when he finds the right girl. I think marriage and moving out on one's own are tougher to handle for someone like Sky. Not for him to handle, but for us. No matter how high functioning he is; he still needs more help than our other children did. There are quite a few things that he needs help with. He knows money pretty well but he needs help with it. Some of the characteristics that make him so endearing: trust, love for all, and a giving heart; also make him vulnerable to being taken advantage of. Like all of our children, we can't protect him from everything. With enough effort and God's help I think we can protect him from most things. We also have a responsibility to do so. Like any precious gift one receives there is a desire to protect. What more of a special gift could one be given, than to be trusted with a special person, such as Sky?

Consider How It Ends

The future is important to everyone; how they will eat, where one will live, what kind of work they will do. What will their family be like? From traveling to many countries around the world on church related mission trips and spending time with what would be considered common people, I have come to believe that we are all basically the same. It seems that everyone pretty much wants the same out of life. We may have different looks, languages and locations but we pretty much all want to live in peace, be healthy, take care of our families, and prosper a little more each year. Our Governments may differ in their thinking from one another but the people don't. Like most people that believe in an afterlife, I care about the short and long term future. We all often wonder exactly where we are going when we die, or wonder where we were before we were born. We all face the same mysteries of life whether we want to think about them or not. I have found a peace in my faith that helps me to not worry about my eternal future. I think having kids, Sky in particular, strengthened my faith in an afterlife and life having a purpose. I many times thought about how nice it would be to be like Sky or many of the Special people like him. Love everyone, have fun at school, not worry about the future, and just live life. I even joked that if I could go back and do school over again, I would find a way to be in Special Education. They didn't have too much school pressure, had lots of fun, and went on a lot of field trips. My schooling wasn't like that. Then that day came when Sky, like so many times before, surprised me with his thoughts. As mentioned earlier it was when Sky told me that he didn't want to die and told me that he was afraid to die. I knew that Sky was fascinated with funerals and death but I really didn't think he thought about it in such a deep way. I assured Skylar that he didn't have to worry about dying. I told him that I would most likely die before him but that he would see me again. I reminded him that he believed like our family does, that if you accept Jesus in your heart you will go to live in Heaven for eternity. I reassured him that he would have other family members to help him when his mother and I were gone, and when he died some day, we would be waiting on him. Someday we would all be together in Heaven and celebrating.

Find Your Purpose

Whatever your place in life or however you believe about an afterlife, I would hope that Skylar's story will inspire you to reflect on your own life and what your purpose is. Everyone, I believe, is put on this earth for a purpose; a God intended great purpose. Most people don't seem to find that purpose or reach their full potential. I'm probably in that group. Though, as I've gotten older, I've tried to find my purpose. People seem to often just get beaten up by life's troubles and distractions; resulting in just trying to get through life. Skylar and others like him seem to serve great purposes although they may not be searching for it. This is particularly true if so called normal people interact with them and get to know them. Skylar has been blessed with many talents, abilities and opportunities that many people don't have. Skylar and I have talked about his purpose in life and his trying to fulfill it. I believe he has a responsibility to help others. The Bible says to whom much is given, much is required. It's a requirement, not an option or expectation. Skylar realizes this and wants to use his gifts and talents to help others and make an impact in this world. Whether you get to meet Skylar in this life or not, I know that he would love to meet you. Better than that, I know that someday Sky would want to meet you in Heaven to celebrate. It's part of his purpose. His purpose is not to just concentrate on life after death matters. It is also to help others to continue doing what we need to be doing while on earth. We need to find and fulfill our purpose and celebrate doing so.

It is Sky and I's desire that whatever your location on this earth or situation in this life, that you can find your purpose and through it learn to live life as a celebratory event. Please join us on this journey of life and also make it your mission to:

CELEBRATE LIFE.

Skylar bringing home the point while delivering his short sermon.

Acknowledgements

It is totally fitting to dedicate this book to Sky's mother and my wife of over 30 years, Paula. She has always been the main caregiver for Skylar as well as our other children. She spent countless days being his advocate and countless nights caring for him through his multiple illnesses. I hoped that she would like the book in its original form. You bet I let her read it. My momma didn't raise no fool. No one will know or needs to know if I had to remove something she considered inappropriate or unfavorable. Likewise, no one will know what I left in that she told me to take out. I love you Paula.

I also need to acknowledge our children, Sky's older siblings: Kristi, Kyle, Colt, and Alexis. You, your spouses, and your children have all loved Skylar unconditionally. You always understood and were never jealous of the time and costs involved to take care of him. I know that he has a loving family that will always take care of him. I love you all.

There are so many others that have been so influential and helpful in Skylar's life, they are too numerous to mention. From Pastors to police officers, from friends to family, from teachers to students, from girlfriends to girl friends, from coaches to caregivers, they have all been placed in Skylar's path for a reason. I am so thankful for each and every one of you. I pray God's special blessing on you for your pouring in to Skylar's life.

Skylar's Short Sermon

(National Fine Arts Festival, August 2014, Columbus, Ohio)

Welcome!

Did you know that nothing is impossible with God?

My name is Skylar Page. I was born a little bit different. Some may think my differences put limits on me, but I'm here to tell you why they don't.

I really love people. I like to help them. I like to talk to people at school, restaurants, church, hotels; Really, I like to talk to people everywhere because I like all people the same. Jesus gave me this desire to love and to help others.

John 15:12 says,
"This is my commandment, that you love one another, just as I have loved you."

Ephesians 2:10 says,
"For, we are God's workmanship, made to do good works, which God made for us to do."

I know it makes God happy when we help others. When I was a baby, I had to have open-heart surgery. I was very sick. People came to visit me, pray for me, and help care for me. This is just one time in my life when people set a Christ-like example for me to help others.

There are many ways to help others. Sometimes, just a few nice words, or a smile is all somebody needs. God gave us all talents. We just need to let him use us.

Try sitting with the kid in the lunchroom that is sitting all by his self.

OR

Try writing a note to your coworker thanking them for showing you the ropes at work.

OR

Try serving food at the home-less shelter in your town.

So many times in our lives we see all of our FAILURES, FEARS, and FLAWS as roadblocks in our lives. I think we put those limits on ourselves. I know that sometimes people look at me and doubt my abilities, but I know that God has a plan for me.

Jeremiah 29:11 says,
"For I know the plans I have for you", says the Lord,"plans to prosper you and not to harm you, plans to give you a hope and a future."

Don't let others or yourself stop you from doing all that you can do.

This May, I graduated from high school. I bet I had doubters, but I know that God never doubted me because he has made me LIMITLESS.

Afterword

I'm sorry to announce it but Skylar didn't pass his Drivers Education class. He did fine on the written portion with my help reading the test questions. I didn't cheat for him and was rather impressed at how well he did. He did pretty good on the driving portion and I could tell he learned a lot. For the final he had to have a driving route memorized and get at least a B grade in order to pass. I had practiced quite a bit with him and thought he would probably pass. I don't know what happened but he must have gotten nervous on the final day. I heard later that he turned the opposite direction of his route when he first left the parking lot. He then just didn't do very well. Rightfully so, the teacher couldn't pass him with a clear conscience. He now has three attempts to pass the driving portion at the local DMV within the next year. The instructor said it is much easier than her final test. I hope he passes but at the same time it brings up a life dilemma either way. If he passes it won't be prudent to allow him to just drive at will. At the same time we will have to try and explain why he can't. I hope we don't have to hide the keys to all of our cars. If he doesn't pass he will be deeply disappointed. It may take away or at least greatly delay a ray of hope in his development and life goals. It makes me sometimes wonder if it was ever a good idea to even let him drive. It's a tough thing to contemplate. Overall, I think we had to try. It gave him hope, a goal to strive for, and I believe inspired others following his attempt.

Sky's restaurant hasn't happened either. We have the land but still don't have the financing for the business concept. The land is now for sale but not because the dream has been given up on. If we could profit a lot on the land, maybe we could pursue the dream at another location. Maybe the timing isn't right. We don't know, but we have to keep trudging forward. Not just for Sky; there is a greater goal. I really believe he has a purpose to help and inspire others. His own business, where he could and would constantly meet and greet people, can be a powerful instrument in fulfilling that purpose.

Sky is still in college. He's still working at Chick-fil-A. Sky is still being Sky; ornery, silly, happy, overtly friendly, smart, intriguing, below average in some folk's eyes, and inspirational in other's.

Sky's still just Celebrating Life.

Skylar Through the Years

Sky age 1

Sky age 2

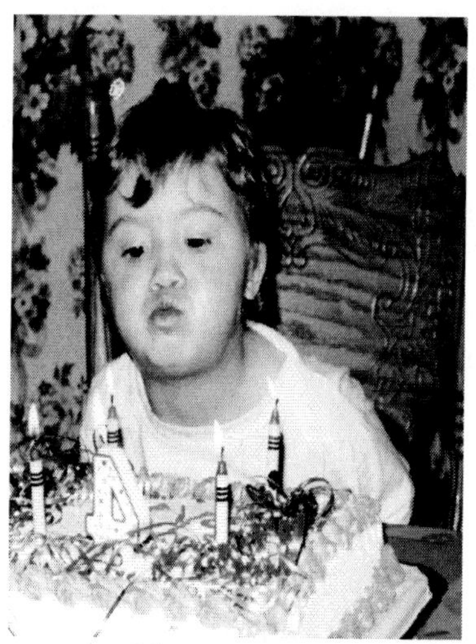

Sky age 4

Sky age 6

Sky age 7

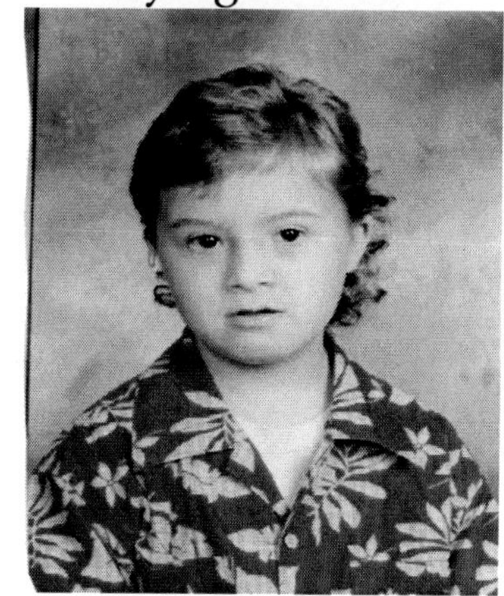

Sky age 9

Sky age 10

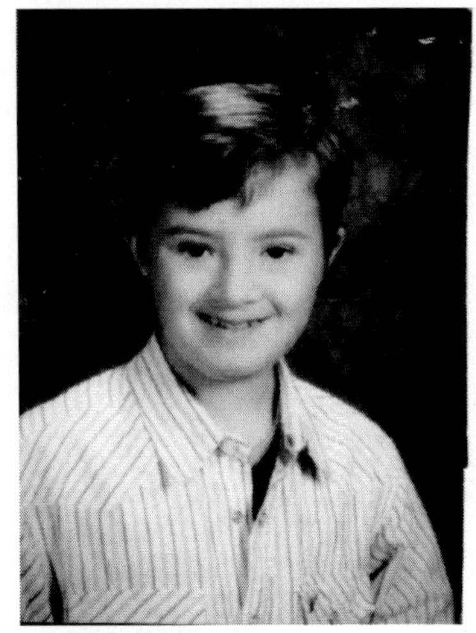

Sky age 11

Sky age 12

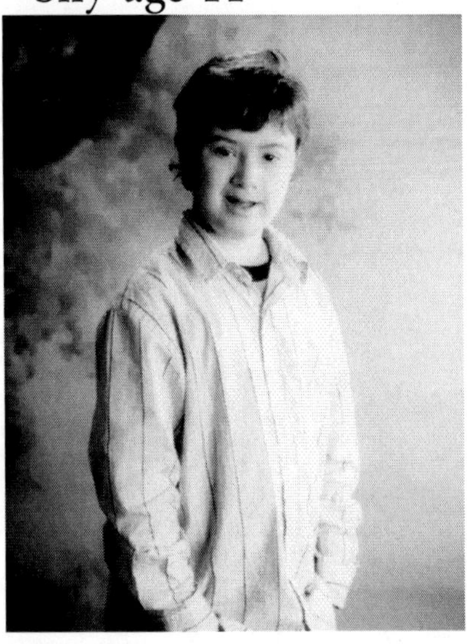

Sky age 13

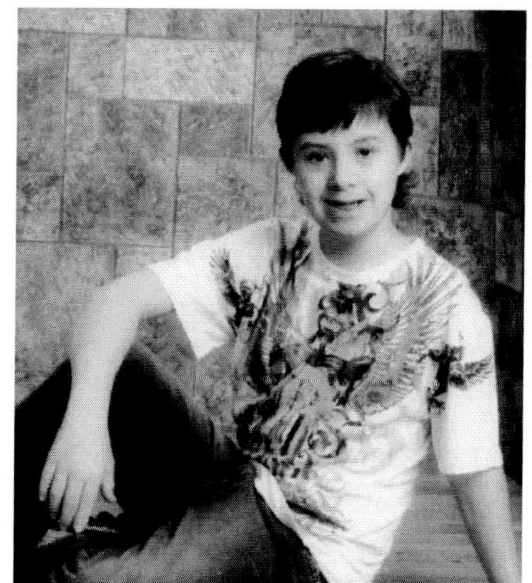

Sky age 14

Sky age 15

Sky age 16

Sky age 17

Sky age 18

Sky age 19

Sky age 20

Sky age 21

Fun Times with Sky

A perfect child

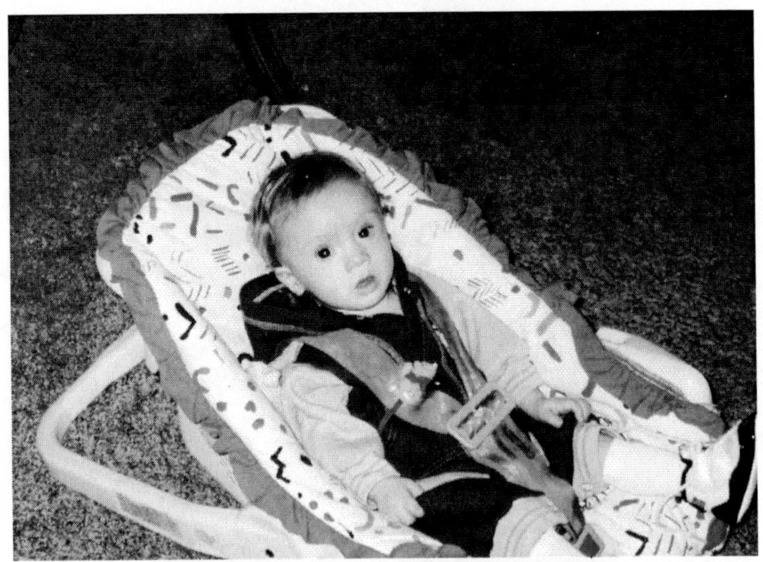

Sky in the faulty carrier that flipped

Having fun

Escape buggy in Washington D.C.

Easter church fun

A gifted young swimmer

Hippo-therapy; I think he just liked horseback riding

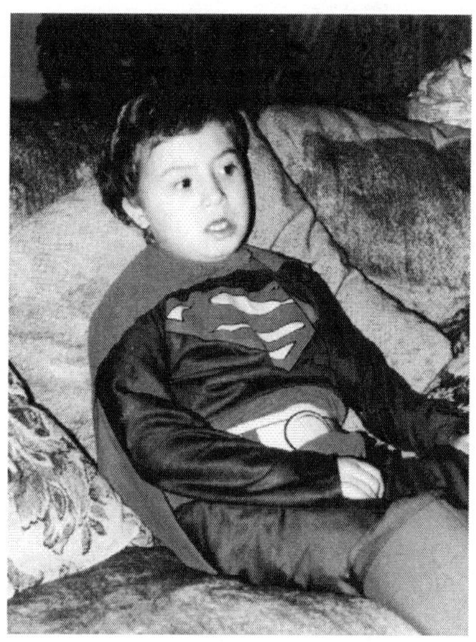

Our Superman

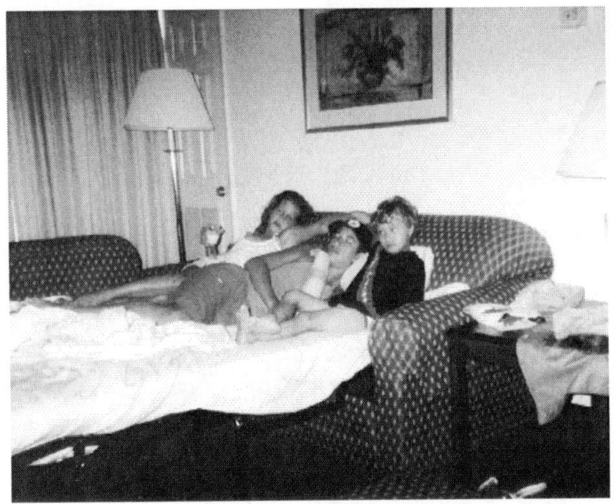

Scene of the hotel room escape

Carrying Sky up Diamond Head, Hawaii

Sky in a Hula Contest, never bashful

Hard to tell who's happiest

Moon face & 23 chicken nuggets

Infamous 17 x 24 bunny ears photo (see mom)

Mutual attraction

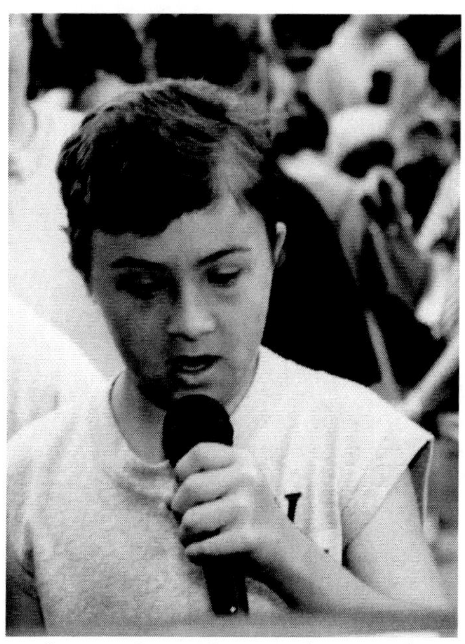

Karaoke of National Anthem, his favorite

European Sky visiting Germany

Styling it in Venice, Italy

World Traveler

New search game, "Where's Sky"

Sky pre-fame on the Jumbo-tron
in Times Square New York City

Skylar at 16 driving a Porsche in a parking lot;
dreaming of future driving I'm sure

Sky ready for a dance

Sky doing Church Missions work
in the Turks Caicos Islands

Sky with his future boss Truett Cathy at the original Chick-fil-A in Hapeville, Georgia

Striking a pose at the Destin, Florida Harbor

OKC Thunder major fan until he became a traitor when KD went to the Warriors

Proving he's a Ladies Man, even practicing with a plastic one

Riding off into the Sunset
What a fitting ending

THE END